The Great Women Chefs
of France

Compiled by
Madeleine Peter

ILLUSTRATED BY RODICA PRATO

TRANSLATED AND EDITED BY
NANCY SIMMONS

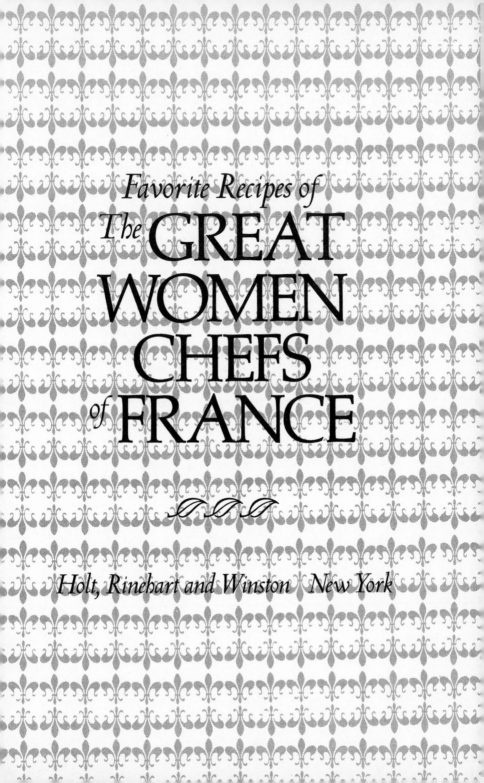

Favorite Recipes of
The GREAT WOMEN CHEFS of FRANCE

Holt, Rinehart and Winston   New York

Library of Congress Cataloging in Publication Data
Peter, Madeleine.
Favorite recipes of the great women chefs of France.
Translation of Grandes dames de la cuisine.
Includes index.
1. Cookery, French. I. Title.
TX719.P47613   641.5'944   79-10799
ISBN 0-03-044311-3

Designer: Joy Chu
Printed in the United States of America
1   3   5   7   9   10   8   6   4   2

TO PAUL SCHMITT

Contents

ANNIE DESVIGNES
La Tour du Roy
45 rue du Général-Leclerc, 02140 Vervins-en-
Thiérache (Aisne), 55 km from Saint-Quentin,
22 km from Hirson (23) 98-00-11. Closed: July.

LUCIENNE DREBET
Chez Georges
8 rue du Garet, 69001 Lyon (78) 28-30-46.
Closed: Saturday, Sunday; August.

JEANNE DROUIN
Auberge du Grand Saint-Pierre
Les Haies à Charmes, 59228 Dourlers (Nord),
N2, 8 km from Avesnes-sur-Helpe (20) 61-17-58.
Closed: Monday.

FERNANDE EUZET
Le Pistou
5 boulevard de Port-Royal, 75013 Paris 707-27-57.
Closed: Saturday, Sunday; July.

MARTHE FAURE
Auberge Saint-Quentinoise
23 avenue de la République, 93190 Livry-Gargan
(Seine-Saint-Denis), 13 km from Aubervilliers
927-13-08. Closed: Monday; August 1–21.

MARIE-JO FERRAND
Gîte-du-Tourne-Pierre
Route de Soullans, 85300 Challans (Vendée)
(51) 68-14-78. Closed: Friday evening, Saturday lunch;
January 1–15, September 1–15.

MARIE-LOUISE JULIEN 163
Hôtel de la Vieille Poste
58230 Ouroux-en-Morvan (Nièvre), 25 km from
Château-Cinon (86) 84-91-11 ext. 47. Closed:
Monday off-season; October 1–15.

LÉA BIDAUT 170
La Voûte
11 place A.-Gourju, 69002 Lyon (78) 42-01-33.
Closed: Saturday, Sunday; July 1–August 15.

ANTOINETTE LÉGER 178
Au Capitaine
5 quai Guiné, 85100 Les Sables-d'Olonne (Vendée)
(51) 32-18-10. Closed: Thursday evening, Friday;
October.

SIMONE LEMAIRE 188
Le Tourne-Bride
Le Pin-au-Haras, 61310 Exmes (Orne), 13 km
from Argentan (34) 67-92-02.
Closed: Wednesday; January 1–March 15.

CHRISTIANE MASSIA 198
L'Aquitaine
54 rue de Dantzig, 75015 Paris 828-67-38.
Closed: Sunday.

COLETTE MAUDONNET 210
Aux Naulets d'Anjou
Rue Croix-de-Mission, 49350 Gennes (Maine-et-
Loire), 15 km from Saumur (41) 51-81-88.
Closed: Monday, January 15–March 1.

Color illustrations fall between pages 14 and 15, 46 and 47, 270 and 271, and 302 and 303.

Preface

Who are the women chefs of France who run restaurants?

I looked for the answer to my question while making a short, regrettably incomplete, tour of France, and I am giving you a book of the information I gathered. It was stimulating. Novice cooks or fearful ones, take heart. Good cooking is less complicated than you imagine.

Try the recipes you will read here. They are transcribed into clear language with no detail omitted. Read the revelations from these women chefs which come out of their own experience. You will see that the products they use aren't rare but that their methods of preparation, full of their own inventions, have created a new style. The most common garden vegetables are used with seafoods, and we are liberated from the potato, which modern industrialization has made tasteless. Their sauces, bound with cold butter, attain a velvetiness and savor one wouldn't guess at. And beurre blanc, with its reputation for being so hard to make successfully, has been tamed. You can launch into making it without anguish.

Working to order, these women do all the traditional long elaborations in double time. With their innate measuring skills they have a special talent in the choice of seasonings, leaving the food with its own taste but enhancing it. All have done nothing but perfect what they have seen around them. There is a tinge of regionalism in their recipes, based in tradition, but rejuvenated by their creative genius. Traditional doesn't mean routine.

Men can acquire their science in schools which prepare them for their career, but to this day women are still not admitted to these schools. They learn "on the job" to perfect their gifts. Some, with connections, learned their work at the restaurant of a confrere, rescued by friendship. There they saw a unit working, breaking down all the skills they had already mastered themselves: the roast chef didn't make sauces; fish and flesh each had a different attendant.

They, our women chefs, hadn't learned to work as part of a unit, to depersonalize their work. The opposite of the men who have the talent to proclaim their merit, the women have remained silent, absorbed by the seriousness of this task which they alone could take on.

Go visit them, these women chefs. Their menus, far from being calcified with their specialties, follow the seasons. They change them nearly every day, keeping their imaginations at the ready for the pleasure of their guests.

Some Notes on Interpreting French Recipes in American Kitchens

✑ ✑ ✑

There are a few basic givens which have not been spelled out in each recipe but should be borne in mind as you cook from this book.

Whenever butter is an ingredient, it means sweet butter. If you use salt butter cut down on the amount of salt in the recipe.

Always remove the bouquet garni before you serve a dish.

In most recipes calling for Gruyère, Swiss (as Emmenthaler is called in this country) is given as an alternative. The preferred cheese would be Gruyère, but not if it is those little processed triangles. If you can't find real Gruyère, use Swiss.

All vegetables which are later going to be eaten (as opposed to aromatics in a stock) should be peeled before being put into the dish to cook.

In recipes calling for rabbit, try to find a very young, small one. French rabbits are smaller than ours. If you buy frozen rabbits they come in two sizes: young and mature. For all the dishes in this book young is preferable.

If crème fraîche is called for in a recipe and is going to be cooked, you can substitute plain heavy cream (preferably not the ultrapasteurized kind). But if you want something more closely approximating French crème fraîche, or if you want to serve it as a garnish, you can make it easily and it will keep in the refrigerator for about 10 days. Then it will turn into heavy sour cream.

Just add 1 teaspoon buttermilk to every cup of heavy cream. Heat to barely warm to your finger, then cover loosely and let stand until it has thickened. Usually overnight will do it unless the weather is very hot or very cold. When it is thick, cover tightly and refrigerate.

In a number of these recipes lard is suggested as a substitute for goose fat. If you use commercial boxed lard it doesn't have much flavor and you may want to add a little bacon fat to the dish to perk it up.

The Great Women Chefs
of France

FERNANDE
ALLARD

⚜⚜⚜⚜

Allard
Paris 6ᵉ

This large, ungraceful, even austere bistro, untouched since
the nineteenth century—the logo of its door emblazoned on
its pots—is the rendezvous for all the gourmets of Paris (and
of the whole world); Allard has seen two wars and two generations of women chefs.

Their formula: quality—the extraordinary savor of the
cooking. Each dish is a finished monument. One can think
of nothing to do to improve it. When a chef raises to the
pinnacle of gastronomy a beef stew with carrots, lamb stew,

coq au vin, pork with red beans, and so many other robust peasant recipes, it is because she adds a good dose of personal genius and of know-how perfected through generations of women cooks.

When Fernande Allard married André (and his bistro) she was no novice. She grew up on one of those Burgundian farms where the least side dish is fit for a king. Her mother, a fine cook, didn't let her palate lie fallow. Fernande formed her taste very young at the family table, and the generous stocks from her mother-in-law's kettles (she is the famous Marthe Allard) crowned her gastronomic faith. She embraced all the family's rites and constraints zealously. One must speak as of a cult, a devotional service in this temple to provincial tradition, where each evening an office is celebrated, an office repeated each week on the plates of its communicants. Monday: cassoulet, Tuesday: coq au vin . . . each day has its ritual. The plats du jour have made this great bistro's reputation.

Fernande's talents didn't stop with these, though. In season game occupies a favored place on the menu. Grouse, pheasants, rabbits, and the rest have their chance to be called sublime by guests and chroniclers.

The desserts are also regal. Traditional chocolate charlotte with custard seems favored by Fernande and the guests over the tarts, the raspberry cake; but look at the gorgeous seasonal fruits served with crème fraîche. To say nothing of the wonderful coffee would be treason. And to ignore the wine cellar would be to forget your homage to André Allard's palate.

TERRINE DE FOIES DE VOLAILLE TRUFFÉE
Chicken liver pâté

𝒯 𝒯 𝒯

FOR A 2-QUART TERRINE

OR 2 BREAD PANS 9 BY 5 BY 3 INCHES

1¼ pounds fresh pork fat
2½ pounds chicken livers
8 eggs
¼ cup cognac
¼ cup port
4 tablespoons thick crème
    fraîche

salt and pepper
nutmeg
allspice
3 truffles
blanched bacon to line the
    terrine and fold over the top
    of the meat

Preheat oven to 350°F.

Chop the pork fat with the chicken livers into very fine bits (or, better yet, put through a meat grinder or food processor). Place in a large bowl and add the eggs one at a time, lightly beaten just to mix, then the cognac and port, the crème fraîche, the salt, pepper, and spices, and the juice from the truffles. Beat with an electric mixer. The mixture should be smooth, soft, fluffy, and well beaten.

Line the mold or molds with slices of blanched bacon long enough so that they can fold over and cover the top of the terrine.

Spoon half the meat into the lined mold. Slice the truffles so that the slices will garnish the whole length of the mold. Arrange them on the meat, then cover them with the rest of the meat mixture. Fold the ends of the bacon over the top and cover with aluminum foil and then a cookie sheet.

The foil shouldn't rest on the meat; it is to help seal in the juices and fat during the cooking.

Place the mold in a large, shallow, ovenproof dish and pour hot (not boiling) water into the larger dish so that it comes about halfway up the sides of the mold.

Place in the preheated oven. Watch to see that the water doesn't boil. If it begins to simmer lower the heat and if necessary open the oven door for a moment. If the water boils it will ruin the texture of the terrine.

After 1 hour test with the point of a knife. The terrine should be pink inside and the juices in the hole made by the knife should also be pink. When the meat is ready, lift off the cookie sheet and the foil and let the terrine rest in a turned-off oven with the door open for 30 minutes.

When you take it out of the oven replace the foil, but again don't let it press on the meat until it has cooled to tepid. Then put a lightish weight on it (such as a paperback book). When the terrine is completely cool refrigerate it, still weighted, for 4–5 hours.

Serve with cornichons. Sliced, the terrine will keep for several days in the refrigerator.

NOTE: Don't let the outrageous price of truffles keep you from trying this recipe. The truffles can easily be omitted. Just add a little (about 1½ tablespoons) sherry to the meat mixture to replace the truffle juice.

PETITE ROUGETS DE ROCHE
AU BEURRE BLANC
Small red mullet with butter sauce

𝒟 𝒟 𝒟

SERVES 6

2 ounces (½ stick) butter
4 tablespoons oil
12 small red mullet

flour
salt and pepper
2 tablespoons chopped parsley

Beurre blanc
2 tablespoons minced shallots
½ cup white wine vinegar
salt and crushed pepper
10 ounces (2½ sticks) butter,
   soft but not melted
1 lemon

Heat the half stick of butter in a large frying pan with the oil. Dredge the fish in flour and cook them quickly in the butter and oil. Drain them on paper towels, then salt and pepper them and arrange them on a serving platter. Sprinkle with chopped parsley. Keep them warm while you make the beurre blanc.

Beurre blanc

Put the minced shallots in a saucepan with the vinegar, salt, and crushed pepper. Reduce slowly until the vinegar is nearly gone. You should end up with a moist shallot paste.

    If you are unsure of your stove use a double boiler for

the next step. But be careful not to let the water in the bottom boil—it should stay at about 190°F.

Bit by bit whisk about a third of the soft butter into the shallot paste, whisking to incorporate after each addition. When the mixture is emulsified add several squirts of lemon juice, another third of the butter, and finally, whisking constantly, the last third. When all the butter has been incorporated, beat for another minute. If you just like the taste of the shallots but don't want the morsels, strain.

Reheat the beurre blanc in a double boiler (it shouldn't get hotter than about 145°F.). Correct the seasoning (remember, beurre blanc should not be bland) and serve in a sauceboat.

BOEUF MODE AUX CAROTTES
Pot roast with carrots

ɍɍɍ

SERVES 6 TO 8

Fernande Allard, backed by the experience of a house filled with many generations of cooks, believes that cooking meat with carrots doesn't improve either one.

2 chicken carcasses
1 carrot
1 leek
2 bouquets garnis (parsley, bay leaf, thyme)
1 tablespoon tomato purée
salt and pepper
goose fat or lard
3-pound strip of rump steak, larded

4 onions, quartered
5 tablespoons cognac
1 bottle dry white wine
2 calves' feet
flour
4½ pounds carrots
4 ounces (1 stick) butter
2 tablespoons chopped parsley

Begin by making a stock: heat 8 cups of water, the chicken carcasses, 1 carrot, the leek, a bouquet garni, and the tomato purée in a large pot. The stock should simmer for 2 hours before you add the beef. Add salt and pepper to taste. Strain, but keep the solids.

Melt 2 tablespoons of fat or lard in a large, very heavy casserole and sear the beef on all sides. Remove it from the pot and in its place add the onions. When they are golden, return the meat to the pot, add salt and pepper, and reheat. Sprinkle with the cognac and flame.

Pour in wine to come two-thirds of the way up the meat, then add chicken stock to cover, and a second bouquet garni. Cover the casserole and let simmer over very low heat for 2 hours. While it is cooking, cut the calves' feet into pieces, scald them, dry them, and after the first 2 hours add them to the casserole. Continue to simmer for another 2 hours.

While the meat is cooking, in another saucepan make a brown roux out of 1 tablespoon fat or lard and 2 tablespoons flour. Cook slowly, stirring constantly so that the roux doesn't burn. Add all the remaining chicken stock along with the strained solid matter. Let it thicken. If necessary add a little wine, but not more than ½ cup. Cook over very low heat for the same 2 hours as the last half of the stew cooking. Strain and press the solids left in the sieve to get the goodness out. Discard what is in the sieve and set the stock aside. You will have a very thick sauce.

Peel the carrots and cut into rounds about ¾ inch long. Cook in a lot of boiling salted water and when they can be pierced easily with a knife but are still crisp, drain. Put in a saucepan with the butter. Don't cook them any more, just salt and pepper and keep warm.

To finish, add a ladleful of stock from the cooking pot to the sauce and let simmer until you are ready to serve.

Serve the meat sliced on a heated serving platter surrounded with the pieces of calves' feet, and the sauce spooned over both. The carrots should be served separately, sprinkled with chopped parsley.

NAVARIN AUX POMMES
Lamb stew with potatoes

SERVES 6 TO 8

3½–4 pounds lamb neck or shoulder, cut into stewing pieces
3–4 tablespoons lard
1 onion, chopped
4 cloves garlic, chopped
2 tablespoons flour
1½ cups white wine (such as Chavignol)
2 cups chicken stock
3 tomatoes, peeled, seeded, and roughly chopped
1 bouquet garni (bay leaf, thyme, rosemary, and parsley)
salt and pepper

Melt the lard in a large frying pan and brown the meat. Remove lamb to a casserole, and in the frying pan, adding more lard if necessary, brown the onion and garlic.

When they are brown add them to the casserole with the meat and sprinkle with the flour. Stir the meat, onions, garlic, and flour together and over low heat brown the flour lightly. Then add the white wine and enough stock to cover the meat. Finish by adding the tomatoes, bouquet garni, and salt and pepper.

Bring the stew to a simmer, then cover and simmer over very low heat for about 3 hours. When it is done, remove the meat to a serving bowl and bring the liquid to a rapid boil. Reduce the liquid until it becomes syrupy, skimming off the fat and foam as it rises to the top. Pour the reduced sauce over the meat and serve with *pommes cocotte*.

Pommes cocotte

$3\frac{1}{2}$–4 pounds potatoes
3 tablespoons lard (or bacon fat
   if you like the taste)
salt and pepper
2 tablespoons chopped parsley

Peel the potatoes and dice them into pieces about $1\frac{1}{2}$ inches square. Put them into a casserole. Add enough water or stock to cover them halfway, then 3 tablespoons lard or bacon fat.

Cook, uncovered, over high heat. The liquid will evaporate and the potatoes will begin to color in about 15 minutes. As soon as that happens lower the heat, add salt and pepper, and, turning the potatoes often, cook them another 15 minutes or so until they are a beautiful golden brown. Serve sprinkled with chopped parsley.

CHARLOTTE AU CHOCOLAT
Chocolate charlotte

ƧƧƧ

SERVES 8

14 ounces bittersweet chocolate
½ cup extra-fine sugar
10 eggs, separated
14 ounces (3½ sticks) butter

15 ladyfingers, split in lengthwise halves
5 tablespoons granulated sugar
kirsch

Choose as pure and dark a chocolate as possible. Break into pieces and place in a large saucepan with ¼ cup of the extra-fine sugar and enough water to cover (probably about ½ to ¾ cup—less is better here). When you have obtained a hot, beautifully glossy liquid, add all the egg yolks at once, stirring over heat as you would a custard. As soon as the mixture comes to the first bubbles of a boil remove from the heat and add the butter in pieces, stirring until it is melted and absorbed.

Beat the whites until they are soft peaks, then add the other ¼ cup extra-fine sugar carefully, continuing to beat. Well-beaten whites should be able to be divided with a knife. Mix the whites into the chocolate. Don't worry about keeping them inflated—it is more important that they be perfectly incorporated.

Spread a piece of waxed paper on a tray and line up the split ladyfingers on it, rounded side down. Make a syrup from the 5 tablespoons of granulated sugar and 2 tablespoons water, and flavor it with kirsch (or any other liqueur or brandy you like). Bring to a boil, let boil for 5 minutes, then remove from the heat.

Flatten the ladyfingers with the palm of your hand, then paint them, using a pastry brush, with the sugar syrup. They should absorb it. Flatten them again and line a 7-cup charlotte mold with them, starting with the bottom. Line the bottom by making a rosette of the ladyfingers, then line the sides, arranging the ladyfingers, rounded sides out, around the mold. Fill the lined mold with the chocolate mixture, then cover the top with another rosette of ladyfingers. Cover with a piece of aluminum foil, but don't press.

Refrigerate for 8 hours, then gently tamp to compress the top.

If you have any chocolate mixture left over, as you probably will, you can put it in a rounded bowl and serve unmolded. This marvelous mousse will last in the refrigerator. Serve with crème anglaise.

Crème anglaise
1 vanilla bean (see note)
⅓ cup sugar
3 cups half-and-half
6 egg yolks

Cut the vanilla bean in half the long way and place it along with the sugar in the half-and-half in a small saucepan. Bring to a boil, then remove from heat and let stand to infuse for a few minutes. Beat together the yolks, just to mix, then little by little pour the scalded liquid through a strainer into the yolks, beating as you pour. When the yolks are incorporated, pour them back into the rest of the strained liquids.

Return to the heat and cook, stirring constantly, without letting the custard boil again, until it has thickened enough to coat a wooden spoon.

Note : In the custard you may substitute vanilla sugar for the sugar and vanilla bean.

PAULETTE
ARBULO

L'Estanquet
Gastes/Parentis-en-Born (Landes)

Paulette Arbulo, known in her family as Pepette, is the daughter of another chef, Georgette Descat.

What she learned in five years in her mother's kitchen—a sense of discrimination, the manual skills, order and organization—have become the basis of her knowledge. Her imagination has led her to experiment; her palate was educated to judge the results. In one year her work became not just Georgette's daughter's but Paulette's.

She is young, alert, and sharp. One can still see in her kitchen manner traces of youthful febrility from the hours at her mother's Lous Landes. But here, in her own Estanquet,

Soupe aux fruits

6 oranges

2 pamplemousses

fraises

framboises

6 œufs

pruneaux

sucre   alcool à l'orange

Homards aux petits légumes

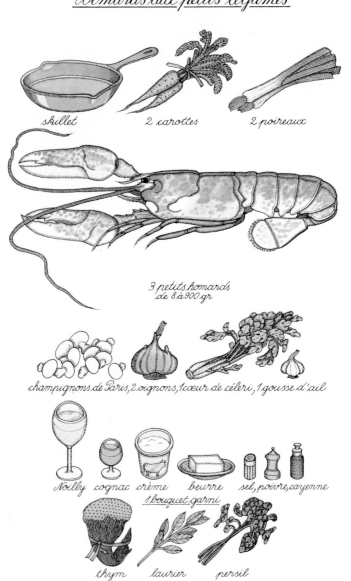

skillet

2 carottes

2 poireaux

3 petits homards
de 8 à 900 gr

champignons de Paris, 2 oignons, 1 cœur de céleri, 1 gousse d'ail

Noilly cognac crème beurre sel, poivre, cayenne

1 bouquet garni

thym laurier persil

she refound the time to live, to watch her twelve-year-old twins at play.

A small house with the entrance on a little square and around it enough space to add a terrace someday, that is Estanquet. Paulette and her husband have been at Gastes for only a short time, but they are not there by chance. Monsieur Arbulo is from the region and Paulette from a bit farther away, but still, definitely Landes.

Their first concern when they arrived was to modernize the interior and install a large kitchen (a reaction against her mother's too-small one in Paris). She soon realized her mistake: she walks miles each day going from the refrigerator to the oven, from the sink to the office. Of course, she can breathe here, she says with a contrite smile.

In Gastes she has known everyone for a long time: the gardeners who have vegetables, the fishermen, the stock farmers, and a friend who puts up prunes for her. A find. The best prunes in Agen, brought in 10-pound cases and divided up into jars. So they are always ready—for a fruit salad, a tart or sherbet, a dish of rabbit with prunes. Or to eat whole, as is, soft and rich with their flavor intact.

Paulette's menu is strongly marked by regionalism. How could it not be in this country of perfect produce? It is the beginning of *garbure* territory—that Basque country broth, rather than soup, of cassoulet, which is nowhere brawnier than here in Languedoc. But the glory of the country is its foie gras and quality chickens.

Paulette has tested her skill on several savory creations: chicken with asparagus, rabbit with prunes, and *granités*, frozen fruits of the season, which can be eaten at any time of day, like an ice.

This young woman is a solid link in the chain of great women chefs.

LE TOURIN DE GASTES

ℐ ℐ ℐ

4 onions

6 cloves garlic

1 tablespoon goose fat

salt and pepper

1 egg

1 generous teaspoon good wine
    vinegar

good white bread for toasting

Mince the onions and the garlic and cook them gently in the
goose fat without letting them take on color. Cover with 8
cups water or a light stock (maybe 2 cups bouillon and 6 cups
water). Add salt and pepper and let cook for 30–40 minutes.

Beat the egg with the vinegar of your choice.

Off the heat beat the egg-vinegar into the boiling liquid.
Serve immediately in a tureen.

Accompany with triangles of toast.

GARBURE LANDAISE
Bean soup

✐ ✐ ✐

SERVES 6 TO 8

1 ham hock
1 pound ham rind or very lean
    bacon
1 medium cabbage
4 carrots
4 leeks

1 head celery
1 tin preserved liver (goose,
    duck, chicken, or pork)
1 pound (hulled weight) fresh
    broad beans (lima, fava, etc.)
salt and pepper

Bring 16 cups of water to a boil, then add the ham hock and
the rind or bacon. Let simmer for 3 hours.

While the pork is cooking, julienne the cabbage (that is,
cut into little strips). Slice the carrots, leeks, and celery into
thin rounds.

When the meat has simmered for 3 hours, add the cabbage, carrots, leeks, and celery and simmer for another hour.
Then add the preserved liver, whichever kind you prefer,
and the fresh beans. Cook another hour.

The cooking, kept very gentle, should last at least 5
hours. Just before serving taste and add salt and pepper (it
probably won't need much salt because of the ham). This
soup is thick enough to serve as a main dish in shallow soup
plates accompanied by triangles of good white toast. Slice the
meats and serve them out into each plate, then spoon the
soup itself over them.

In winter use dried beans but soak them for 2–3 hours

17

first. Add them with the rest of the vegetables. Home-preserved beans are better though, and if you have them add them with the preserved liver.

The quality of the aroma at the presentation of this soup —real comfort food—is dependent on the slowness of the cooking.

POULET AUX ASPERGES
Chicken with asparagus

✐✐✐

SERVES 6

3½-pound chicken
1 onion
2 carrots
2 leeks
1 bouquet garni (parsley, thyme, bay leaf)

2–2½ pounds asparagus (see note)
4 egg yolks
1 tablespoon wine or cider vinegar
salt and pepper

Carve the chicken as though it were cooked. In the refrigerator set aside the wings, the breast fillets, the legs, second joints, and any other meat parts.

Use the carcass to make a stock. Put it into a large, fairly deep pot with the giblets and neck of the chicken. Add the onion, carrots, leeks, bouquet garni, and about 6 cups of water. Let cook for 20 minutes or so.

Peel the asparagus so that the whole stalk is edible (you may have to go quite deep at the stem end), then tie the stalks into small, neat bundles, about eight to a bundle. Put the bundles into the chicken stock with the tips up and out of the liquid. They are tenderer and will steam as the stems boil. Let cook for about 10–15 minutes or until done.

Remove the asparagus and set aside to keep warm. Strain the stock, then return it to the stove and simmer. Put the reserved chicken pieces into the stock and cook them until they can be pierced easily with a fork—about 20 minutes.

Set aside the chicken with the asparagus and keep warm

but don't let them continue cooking. If they seem to be drying out, moisten them with a little stock. They will heat up again when you serve them with the sauce.

Strain the stock again and return to the stove. Bring it to a rapid boil and reduce it to about $1\frac{1}{2}$ cups. Beat the egg yolks with the vinegar.

When the stock has reduced remove it from the heat and beat the yolks and vinegar into it, using a wire whisk. Return to the heat. Let the sauce thicken without coming to a boil, stirring constantly. It is ready when it is the consistency of a thin cream sauce and coats a wooden spoon.

Correct the seasoning.

Arrange the chicken and asparagus on a serving platter and cover them with the sauce. Serve on hot plates.

NOTE: If asparagus is not in season you may substitute frozen or canned asparagus or fresh green beans.

MAGRETS À LA FICELLE DESCAT
Duck breast fillets à la Descat

JJJ

SERVES 6

Tomato sauce

2¼ pounds tomatoes
2 onions
3 cloves garlic
2 stalks celery
4 carrots, grated

1 pinch thyme
1 heaping tablespoon goose or
   chicken fat
salt and pepper

Peel and seed the tomatoes.

Chop the onions, garlic, and celery and add them, with the grated carrots and thyme, to the hot goose fat. Cook, covered, for 20 minutes. Add the tomatoes and let cook, uncovered, until mixture reduces to a paste. Put in a blender for a moment, add salt and pepper to taste, and serve hot in a sauceboat.

1 small curly cabbage

Stuffing for cabbage

10 ounces prosciutto or
   unsmoked bacon
4 slices stale white bread
3 chicken livers
2 eggs

Consommé

1½ pounds spareribs
2 turnips, peeled
3–4 carrots, peeled
1 cucumber

2 celery hearts
2 leeks
3–4 small zucchini
sale and pepper

4 large duck breasts (8 fillets)

Take the cabbage apart and blanch the leaves in boiling water until they are supple as tissue—no longer. Lay them out flat on towels.

Prepare the stuffing by putting the prosciutto or bacon, bread, and livers into a blender or processor. They must be very finely minced. Add salt, pepper, and the eggs.

Put a bit of stuffing on each cabbage leaf and wrap the leaves around it to make packages about the size of tangerines. Tie them up with white string.

Put the spareribs for the consommé in 12 cups of cold water in a large kettle and skim it constantly as it comes to the boil. Let it cook for 1 hour, then add the packages of cabbage leaves. Cook over very low heat, barely simmering, for 30 minutes. While it cooks prepare the vegetables. Cut the turnips and carrots into ½-inch rounds, and the cucumber in half. Tie the celery into bundles and the leeks, likewise. Add them to the consommé. The zucchini (left whole) should be added last and shouldn't cook for more than 3–4 minutes before the duck fillets are added. All the vegetables should be a bit undercooked, so they don't fall apart.

Just before you are ready to serve, tie the duck fillets together with string and drop them into the boiling consommé. Let them cook for 4 minutes. They should still be bloody.

To serve, remove the string from the fillets and arrange them on a platter so they overlap and surround them with the nicely arranged vegetables. Accompany with the reduced tomato sauce.

NOTE : Duck fillets are a bit like small steaks, so although Paulette Arbulo suggests serving them rare, you can revise the cooking time to suit your own tastes.

LAPIN AUX PRUNEAUX
Rabbit with prunes

✐ ✐ ✐

12–15 prunes
1 fine, fleshy young rabbit,
   3–4 pounds
1 tablespoon goose fat or lard
3 carrots
2 onions

1 sprig thyme, or ½ teaspoon
   dried
salt and pepper
1 cup dry white wine
1 cup beef stock

Buy the fattest prunes you can find. The ones that come in jars are better for this recipe, but if you can only get the dried ones, soak them in warm water for 2 hours before cooking them.

Cut the rabbit into serving pieces. This is an unfamiliar anatomy, but you will see that the easiest and most natural way to cut is two pieces for each hind leg, two for the breast, and four for the saddle and the two front legs—one piece on each side with the ribs and one with the front leg. Brown the pieces in the fat in a large casserole over low heat. Be careful not to let the fat burn. Slice the carrots into thin rounds and mince the onions and add them to the rabbit. Add the thyme. Cover and cook very slowly, so that the aromatics give off all their sweetness—for about 1 hour. Add salt and pepper.

Stir in the wine and stock, cover, and bring to a boil. Then add the prunes, lower the heat to as low as possible, and cook for another 30–40 minutes.

Serve very hot.

Fresh buttered noodles are the best accompaniment for this.

N o t e s : If you cannot find a butcher who can supply you with fresh rabbit, there are good frozen half rabbits, already cut into pieces, sold boxed. Your butcher should be able to order those for you. You will need two boxes for this recipe.

Rabbits are quite tough and can be tenderized only by longish cooking in liquid, so be sure the stock and wine cover the pieces in the casserole. If 2 cups doesn't quite do it, add more.

CASSOULET DES LANDES
Landes cassoulet

𝒮 𝒮 𝒮

"Cassoulet" is a fighting word in the southwest of France. Each housewife has *her* recipe, *her* method, which is the right, the only way.

Madame Arbulo, too, specifies in giving this savory recipe that it is *hers*.

2 pounds thin-skinned dried white beans	1 small ham hock
	salt and pepper
1 sprig thyme	4 pure pork smoked sausages
2 onions	6 slices smoked pork
1 whole head garlic (unpeeled)	6 slices preserved goose
3–4 carrots	

Soak the beans 6–8 hours. Throw out the water and put the beans in a large pot of fresh, cold water with the thyme; set over low heat so the water barely simmers. When the water does begin to simmer add the onions, garlic, carrots, and ham hock. Cook for 1½ hours.

This is only the first part of the cassoulet. At this point add salt and pepper to taste.

Remove the onions, the head of garlic, the thyme, carrots, and any excess cooking liquid. But reserve it, in case.

Add the sausages, pork, and preserved goose.

Cook for another 30 minutes. If necessary, add a spoonful or two of the reserved cooking water. The cassoulet should be soft but not wet.

LILIANE
BENOÎT

❧❧❧❧❧

Le Soubise
Soubise (Charente-Maritime)

Young, slender, elegant, smiling Liliane Benoît returns from the market, with the springy step of a professional tennis player.

Don't think that her blue slacks, her well-cut white jacket with impeccable lapels, are her going-out clothes. You would find her dressed this way in her kitchen with knives and cleavers in her hands, cutting things apart and trimming the side of meat that she has chosen herself at the slaughter-house.

In the middle of a region rich with all the fruits of the

sea, with vegetable gardens, stock farms and dairy products in abundant quality, she nonetheless raised a pig on a neighboring farm: he never ate anything but scraps from her kitchen. His quality lard and his flesh give her pâtés and terrines a finesse that leaps out at the palate.

In her spare moments the indefatigable Liliane Benoît fills her larder with preserved duck and foie gras straight from Tartas or from a Landais farm famous for raising fowl, which sells its produce exclusively to her.

If her menu, changed after each trip to market, follows the order of the seasons, it also shows that essentially she is a fantasist. It is full of discoveries, of personal interpretations in the preparation of the produce.

One must taste her fish stew, her Charentais chicken, her sole grilled on seaweed, and her maréchal sauce (without onions)—homage to that man from Soubise whose now-forgotten exploits are modestly recalled in an onion purée.

Le Soubise is the work of both Benoîts. Monsieur Benoît, René to his intimates, takes care of the administration. He is "steward," as his wife says. He is also a man with a talent as an elegant pastry chef and has another even more precious talent: he is a sommelier with a cellar of more than five thousand bottles.

SOUPE AUX MOULES
Mussel soup

1¾ pounds trimmings from any white fish (sole, merlan, etc.—see note)
5–6 pounds medium mussels
1 bouquet garni (thyme, parsley, bay leaf)
2 ounces (½ stick) butter

2 tablespoons flour
salt and pepper
1 egg yolk
3 tablespoons heavy cream
1 lemon
chopped fresh parsley or chervil

Make a stock of the fish trimmings (heads, backs, etc.) and the bouquet garni in 2 quarts of water. Let it cook slowly for 30 minutes.

While it is cooking steam open the mussels. Put them in a large pot with about 2 cups of water and cook, covered, just until they open. Discard any mussels that don't open. Remove the mussels from their shells but reserve the liquid they were steamed in. Set it aside, and the sand and dirt will sink to the bottom.

Strain the fish stock and add the clear part of the mussel liquor to it. (Be careful not to get any sand in.) Cream the butter with the flour and stir into the bouillon.

Correct the seasoning and bring to a boil, stirring constantly with a wire whisk. Beat the egg yolk into the cream, add several squirts of lemon juice, and whisk that into the soup, too, stirring constantly. Don't let the soup come to a boil again.

Divide the mussels among heated serving bowls, then fill each bowl with the soup (which should be creamy). Serve very hot sprinkled with chopped parsley or chervil.

N o t e : Instead of making a white fish stock you can substitute 3 cups of clam juice. If you have made this soup ahead of time, reheat the mussels in the soup before serving.

SAUCE MARÉCHAL

ℐ ℐ ℐ

SERVES 4
MAKES ABOUT I CUP

This is a beurre blanc with lots of flavorings to use on all seafoods. It is particularly good on sole, striped bass, or grilled lobster.

1 heaping tablespoon minced shallots

1 tablespoon chopped parsley

1 level teaspoon thyme

¼ bay leaf, crushed

1 small branch fresh fennel, or 1 teaspoon fennel seeds

2 or 3 large basil leaves, crushed

1 teaspoon green peppercorns, crushed

1 cup dry white wine

1 large pinch salt

10 ounces (2½ sticks) fresh butter, at room temperature

1 lemon

Combine all ingredients except the butter and lemon in a small saucepan. Cook, reducing slowly, until they are almost a paste. Strain and press on the residue in the sieve to extract all the juices. You should end up with about 2 tablespoons essence.

Cut the butter into walnut-sized pieces. Return the essence, with three or four bits of butter, to the saucepan and cook over very low heat. Stirring constantly with a whisk, keep adding pieces of butter, bit by bit, until it is all incorporated. As you add the butter also add squirts of lemon juice.

The sauce should be smooth and slightly thick, somewhat thicker than heavy cream.

Watch out that you don't let it get too hot—that would make the butter burn.

If the sauce must wait, let it go cold rather than trying to keep it in a double boiler. Reheat carefully when you are ready to use it. It is very fragile.

LA CHAUDRÉE CHARENTAISE
Charentaise fish stew

        𝒟 𝒟 𝒟

SERVES 6

This is a fish stew/soup from Charente-Maritime.

2 sole, each 10 ounces
2 large sea robins
3 whiting
3 small eels
1 quart mussels
4 cuttlefish or 4 medium squid
4 ounces (1 stick) butter, quite
  cold and hard

4 cloves garlic, quartered
1 bottle dry white wine
1 bouquet garni (thyme,
    parsley, bay leaf)
salt and pepper

Ask your fish man to fillet the sole and return the trimmings to you. Also ask him to clean the other fish and save you the heads and scraps.

Cut each fish into three or four pieces. Separate them into categories so you can cook them one after the other and all will arrive at the table firm. The first to go into the pot will be the sea robins, then the sole, the whiting, and the eels, and finally the mussels. Scrub the mussels carefully: they will open in the cooking liquid at the end of the preparation.

Cut the whites of the cuttlefish or the tentacles of the squid into strips. Cook in a large kettle in 1 tablespoon butter over moderate heat until they stiffen. When they are firm but haven't taken on any color add the garlic and the heads and trimmings of the fish. Stir for several minutes. When everything is hot, moisten with a mixture of 2 cups wine and 4 cups water. Add the bouquet garni and cook for 20–25 minutes at a gentle boil. Add salt and pepper.

Remove the heads and trimmings and add the fish in the order indicated. Allow several minutes between additions. One way to judge is when, after each addition, the stock returns to the quiver just before the boil, add the next batch. Never let the soup come to a full boil. This will not only preserve the flesh of the fish, it will also ensure that they are perfectly cooked.

Remove the fish with a slotted spoon, arrange them in a tureen, cover, and keep them warm. Strain the broth, then return it to the heat and bring to a full boil. Toss in the mussels, all at once, then remove the pot from the heat and cover. After several minutes the mussels will open. Remove them from the soup and arrange them in the tureen with the fish. Return the soup to a boil and correct the seasoning. Off the heat add the remaining butter in small pieces, whisking vigorously. When it is all incorporated, spoon the soup over the fish and serve instantly.

Slices of good toast are an excellent accompaniment to this handsome, hearty preparation.

POULET À LA CHARENTAISE
Chicken charentaise

S S S

SERVES 4

This recipe, invented and presented for the Poêle d'Or by Madame Benoît, was a finalist in that contest.

2½–3-pound chicken
1 egg
salt and pepper
1 tablespoon Pineau de
   Charentes (see note)

about ¾ cup flour
about ¾ cup white bread
   crumbs (see note)
1 tablespoon butter
3 tablespoons oil

Sauce
2 cups heavy cream
4 egg yolks
⅓ cup Pineau de Charentes
salt and pepper

Accompaniments
4 tart firm cooking apples,
   peeled and cored
2 ounces (½ stick) butter

Peel and core the apples and put them in a small, ovenproof dish. Put a tablespoon of butter on each and place in a 300°F. oven for 40 minutes. They can be cooking while you prepare the rest of this dish.

For this recipe you want to cut the chicken apart and bone it without cutting into the flesh any more than necessary. Cut off the two legs with their second joints and the wings with the breast fillets. This is most easily done if you start cutting at the tip of the breastbone and slice parallel to the rib cage on one side until you get to the joint holding the second joint to the body. Cut through the joint and remove the leg in one piece. Then cut down in the front until you get to the joint attaching the wing to the body. Cut through that and remove the wing with the breast fillet. Do the same on the other side. Discard the carcass or save it to make stock, but you won't need it for this recipe.

You will have four largish pieces of chicken. Cut off and discard the wing tips. From the inside of the meat cut along the leg bone and the wing bone and scrape the flesh away. Discard both bones. Remove the skin from all pieces. Now you will have four pieces of pure chicken flesh. Cut eight pieces of waxed paper and put each piece of chicken between two. Pound with a mallet or a heavy bottle to flatten as you would a veal scallop.

Beat the egg with a fork just to mix, then beat in salt and pepper and lighten with a tablespoon of the Pineau. Dredge each piece in the flour, then in the egg. Roll each piece up as you would a rug, with the neatest part on the outside, and coat with the crumbs, making sure they stick.

In a large skillet heat the butter and oil together over low heat. Arrange the chicken rolls in the pan so they don't touch each other and cook slowly, uncovered. Turn the chicken from time to time as a side browns so it will color evenly. When the crusts are uniformly golden the chicken should be cooked.

Sauce

Heat the cream in a saucepan so that it reduces to half. Cook over moderate heat; it must keep its aroma and color.

Beat the yolks with the ⅓ cup Pineau and the salt and pepper to mix well. When the cream is reduced, pour a little of the hot cream slowly into the beaten eggs, beating constantly; then, still beating, pour back into the rest of the cream. Cook, watching the heat carefully, until the sauce thickens and will coat a spoon. It must not boil.

Serve the chicken without its cooking juices, surrounded by apples, and with the sauce spooned over it.

Serve with a spicy salad.

NOTES: If you don't want to go to the trouble of boning a chicken for this recipe (although that makes the dish more interesting) you can substitute suprêmes, boned chicken breasts—two to a person.

White bread crumbs for the coating are made from stale white bread, ground fine in a blender. Use good, firm-textured bread to get good crumbs which will brown beautifully. Make the crumbs a bit ahead so they will be perfectly dry when you use them.

Pineau, a sweet, fortified wine from Cognac, is a bit hard to find, and you can substitute any sweet white wine with a spoonful of cognac added.

MADAME DE BERNARD

Château de Teildras
Cheffes-sur-Sarthe
(Maine-et-Loire)

Between Loire and Brittany, on the banks of the Sarthe, is a charming château, Teildras, fashioned by the centuries, each of which has left on it the mark of its own style. It is the home of a family who have opened it to the public, transforming it into an elegant inn.

Madame de Bernard de Breil is modest. She judges her talents to be within reach of all intelligent women with a taste for work well done and great zeal, imagination, talent, generosity—and a lot of knowledge.

In her own kitchen this small woman of steel, beautifully turned out from morning on, like the *directrice* of a couturier house, reveals her personality. Her work is a well-ordered ballet. Assisted by a young student from the hotel school, she prepared, before my eyes, two dishes for the dinner menu.

"My menus are simple. I leave the method of preparation of the meat to the guests. They often choose broiled, so the accompaniments have to provide interest. We have a first-rate butcher here, and in hunting season furred and feathered game is available. But most of all we have our abundant rivers. Fruits and vegetables, all top quality, are plentiful, too.

"I make my desserts myself. My ice creams and sherbets are made with fresh fruits, as are my tarts. The pastry is never fine enough to suit me. The tarts are cooked during the meal and served warm with a big bowl of farm cream. There is also chocolate mousse, because men like it, and in winter my *cassonade* tart.

"I personally hardly ever depart from the traditional, but I have observed a new youthfulness, if one can say that, in the delicacy of the cooking and in the rediscovery of the most modest garden vegetables. Leeks, carrots, and spinach are now eaten by everyone, sautéed in good butter, poached in flavored stocks, gratinéed, and so on.

"We entertain many foreigners who visit France making short stopovers, and who all wish to discover the traditional French cooking. Better than the most eloquent guides, cooking shows them our patrimony, our customs, our daily life."

POTAGE VELOUTÉ DE LÉGUMES
Creamy vegetable soup

✐ ✐ ✐

ABOUT 13 CUPS

4 fat leeks
1 celeriac, the size of a man's
  fist, peeled and thinly sliced
6 carrots, thinly sliced

1 medium cauliflower
4 ounces (1 stick) butter
salt and pepper
½ cup heavy cream (optional)

Slice the whites of the leeks (and a bit of the green) into small rounds. Rinse well to get rid of all soil. Dry.

Place the leeks with half the butter in a 4-quart soup kettle over low heat. Let them soften, but don't let them color. Add the celeriac and carrots. When all the vegetables are hot, pour in 9 cups of boiling water. Then add the cauliflower, either whole (if it will fit) or broken into flowerets. Bring the liquid back to a boil, then lower the heat so that it maintains a slight simmer. Too strong a boil would be injurious to the delicacy of this soup.

When all the vegetables are perfectly cooked (about 20 minutes), be sure they don't cook any more. Immediately grind the vegetables in a blender or a processor or put them through a food mill. Then strain the liquid back into the pot through a fine sieve and regrind the strained vegetables until they are the consistency of not-quite-ready cream of wheat. Return them to the liquid in the pot. What you will have is a fragrant, delicate velouté, which requires neither flour nor eggs as a binding agent. Season with salt and pepper.

To serve bring the soup back to a boil, then immediately take it off the heat, beating to mix it well. Serve in cups with a lump (just under a tablespoon in each cup) of butter, accompanied by several slices of toast.

If you want to use cream, a teaspoon in each cup is about right to replace the butter.

TERRINE DE POISSON CHAUDE
Hot fish pâté

ℐ ℐ ℐ

FOR A 12-INCH CAKE PAN

This pâté is made with white fish such as pike or perch, some used very finely chopped, raw, and the rest cut into not-so-fine dice and stiffened in butter. The beautiful, aromatic flesh is suspended in a pâte à choux. It is served hot with a creamy beurre blanc flavored with herbs of the season.

The fish

4 ounces (1 stick) butter	1½ pounds white fish
2 tablespoons minced shallots	(½ pound chopped very fine,
2 tablespoons minced parsley	1 pound diced in pieces about
juice of ½ lemon	½ inch across)
8 ounces mushrooms, minced	1¼ cups dry white Anjou wine

Heat 2 tablespoons of the butter. Add the shallots and cook, stirring often, over moderate heat until they are a paste. Don't let them take on color. When they are cooked, add the parsley and set aside.

Melt another 2 tablespoons of butter in a frying pan, add the lemon juice and the mushrooms, and cook until all the excess moisture has evaporated.

Add the shallots and the chopped (not the diced) fish with ¾ cup of the wine. Stir together and cook until you have a mixture with a mousselike texture. Remove from the heat.

Pâte à choux

4 ounces (1 stick) butter
1 teaspoon salt
3 grinds white pepper
1 pinch grated nutmeg
1 cup flour

3–4 eggs, depending on their
size
1¾ cups heavy cream
juice of ½ lemon

In a large saucepan bring 1 cup of water, 4 ounces of butter, the salt, pepper, and nutmeg to a boil. When the liquid rises and froths, add the flour all at once. Stirring constantly with a wooden spoon, continue to cook until the mixture comes away from the sides of the pot and the spoon. Remove from the heat, stir a bit more, then add the eggs, one at a time, blending each one in well. When the eggs have all been absorbed, continue to work the pâte to get a good consistency: supple and elastic but not soft. The lightness of the cooked pâté will depend on how this is done.

Mixing

Transfer both mixtures to a large, deep bowl and add the cream and the lemon juice. Beat to get a fine paste, the consistency of cream cheese. Melt the remaining 2 ounces of butter and cook the diced fish just until the pieces are stiff, then moisten with the remaining ½ cup of Anjou wine. Add to the bowl with the other ingredients, then taste and correct the seasoning. It should be a bit spicy.

Preheat the oven to 370°F.

Butter a 12-inch cake pan heavily and flour it lightly. Pour the fish pâté into it; it should fall in sheets. Cover with a piece of aluminum foil and place in a bain marie with hot, but not boiling water. Cook for 1½ hours. Check occasionally and don't let the water boil. If it looks as though it might, lower the heat.

Test for doneness by piercing with the point of a knife. When it comes out clean the pâté is done. Let cool in the pan while you make the beurre blanc.

Beurre blanc

1 tablespoon minced shallots   10 ounces (2½ sticks) butter
1 cup dry white Anjou wine   salt and pepper
juice of ½ lemon   fresh chervil or chives, cut up
6 tablespoons heavy cream   with scissors

Have everything ready before you begin: the shallots minced, the butter cut into tablespoon-size pieces, the lemon juiced, and the chosen herb cut up. Cook the shallots in the white wine in the top of a double boiler over direct heat until all the liquid has evaporated. Place over the bottom of the double boiler filled with hot but not boiling water. Add several drops of lemon juice, about a teaspoon of the cream, three or four pieces of butter, salt and pepper, and then a few more drops of lemon juice.

Whisk as you would a mayonnaise until the sauce emulsifies—that is, until the mixture has become opaque and a unified whole. As soon as this happens begin adding the butter, three or four pieces at a time, whisking constantly, so that the mixture remains emulsified. Add the lemon juice in two or three additions as you add the butter. Meanwhile heat the rest of the cream with the cut-up herbs.

Finally, when the sauce is the consistency of mayonnaise, slowly add the heated cream, stirring constantly with the whisk. The sauce should be smooth; if necessary add more cream.

This sauce should be served warm, not hot.

Unmold the pâté onto a heated plate and spoon a moderate

amount of the sauce over it. Serve the remaining sauce in a sauceboat.

This beautiful, delicious preparation can be made even simpler. Cook the pâté the day before you plan to serve it, then reheat in a bain marie filled with *warm* water for at least an hour before serving. Only the sauce has to be made at the last minute.

NOTE: This can also be made in a soufflé dish or another kind of deep dish, but if your container is small and high rather than large and flat you must increase the cooking time accordingly. Your best insurance is the knife-point test. If the point of the knife comes out clean, the pâté is done.

TARTE À LA CASSONADE
Almond tart

✇ ✇ ✇

FOR A 10-INCH CAKE PAN

Pastry
4 ounces (1 stick) butter
⅓ cup sugar
1 pinch salt
1 egg
2 cups sifted flour

Cream the butter, sugar, and salt, using your hands. Add the egg and knead until the mixture is homogeneous. Add the flour all at once and mix rapidly and roughly.

Turn the dough out onto a table and knead by stretching it out under your palm. This is called *fraiser* and helps the dough absorb the flour.

Make a heap of the dough, then cut it into quarters. Pile the pieces one on top of the other, pressing so they stick together. Do this three times. Wrap the dough in waxed paper and set aside in the refrigerator for an hour.

Lightly butter and sugar a 10-inch cake pan. Preheat the oven to 450°F.

Roll out the dough very thin and place it in the buttered and sugared pan. Cover the pastry with aluminum foil, then fill the lined shell with dried beans or rice (make sure there are a lot around the edges of the pan to hold the sides of the dough up). Prick the pastry several times through the foil with the point of a knife.

Turbotin Dugléré

2 carottes   thym   3 poireaux

6 turbotins

persil

vin blanc   poivre   eau

cerfeuil

Dugléré

crème   beurre

2 œufs   3 tomates   3 échalotes

Chou farci

marmite

1 gros chou frisé

Farce

2 oignons   ail   œuf   pain de campagne, sel, poivre

jambon de pays   lard gras   échine de porc

Cuisson

4 carottes   4 poireaux   sel   poivre

petit salé   jarret de porc   4 saucisses de Toulouse

Place in preheated oven. When the crust is firm and the sides look as though they won't slip down (about 5 minutes) remove the foil and the beans or rice. Lower the oven to 350°F. and finish cooking—another 5 minutes—being careful not to let the pastry brown. After removing the crust from the oven, raise the heat to 375°F. to cook the filling.

Filling

1¼ cups brown sugar
⅓ cup ground almonds
4 ounces (1 stick) butter, softened
2 generous tablespoons crème
    fraîche
2 egg yolks

Mix the first four ingredients to make a smooth paste, then beat in the egg yolks, and pour into the cooked pastry shell, smoothing the surface if necessary. Bake in a 375°F. oven for about 15 minutes.

When you check at the end of 15 minutes the filling won't look set—it will still be liquid—but if a skin has formed it is done. Don't let it cook any longer or it will bubble and burn. This filling will set more as it cools, but will never get hard.

Keep this exquisite pastry dough in mind—it goes well with any fruits that don't need cooking, such as strawberries, raspberries, or boysenberries in syrup. It is also perfect with creamy fillings that cook quickly. And the leftover scraps of dough make excellent sugar cookies.

MADAME
CARTET

⚜⚜⚜

Restaurant

Cartet

Paris 11ᵉ

Tradition is worshiped here. From hors d'oeuvres to dessert one might be in the home of a grandmother from Bresse.

But the cook isn't a grandmother: she is a *mère* from the line of those Lyonnaise women who make everything themselves.

Madame Cartet's minuscule restaurant, whose walls are

lined with wood, assures a welcome silence—welcome because it is so rare. That is she, draped with dignity, passing by your table with the menu and returning to serve you.

Although the service is a bit slow, follow Madame Cartet's suggestions and everything will arrive on time.

What one learns from her, rather than recipes, are hints. For example, her beef à la ficelle is served with a ring of marrow bones. Her tripe is marinated in salt and pepper for eight hours before cooking. Consider her shoulder of pork which she puts together in a simmering stew with lentils rather than subjecting it to the tumult of boiling. "Boiling discolors it," she says. The other cured meats that accompany it are placed, still salted, in a big kettle of cold water with the usual aromatics—onion, carrots, a bouquet garni, etc.—and maintained at no more than a simmer, so they can cook, unattended, for two or three hours, depending on their size. And the meat that comes to your plate is pink, soft, and fragrant, accompanied by vegetables cooked to perfection, whether they are dried or fresh.

Madame Cartet's menu includes several specialties that have become rare in Paris, such as sheep's feet *poulette*, or her personal dishes, such as a gratin of seafood, or duck with figs or peaches according to the season, and with oranges in any season.

It is a pleasure to encounter the cheese platter accompanied by nuts, raisins, and slices of buttered toast. The coffee, sipped while crunching on a true Lyonnaise sweet, is always a joy. And finally there is a surprise: a grandfather's digestive drink, "L'Arquebuse." Irresistible.

GRAS-DOUBLE LYONNAISE
Tripe cooked in red wine

ॐ ॐ ॐ

2½ pounds fresh tripe
6 tablespoons lard
2 cups Calvados
3 onions, chopped

3 tomatoes, peeled, seeded, and
  chopped
salt and pepper
1 bottle rough red wine

Cut the tripe into thin strips, drop them into 2 quarts of boiling water, let the water return to the boil, then cook for 10–12 minutes. Drain and dry the tripe, add salt and pepper, and set aside to macerate in a nonmetal bowl for about 8 hours, stirring three times.

Drain and dry the tripe again, then brown the pieces in a large skillet with half the lard until they are golden. Flame with the Calvados, and while the fire is going, shake the pan slightly. (Watch out when you light the match—this is a lot of alcohol, and it will flame up quite high.)

Melt the rest of the lard in a large casserole and cook the chopped onions over medium-low heat. When they are beginning to brown, add the tomatoes, then the tripe with its pan juices, and more salt and pepper—use quite a bit of pepper. Cover and cook over medium-low heat for 1½ hours, stirring often. Add the wine until it comes level with the tripe.

Cover and simmer on low heat for at least another 2½ hours, stirring occasionally. Watch that the tripe doesn't stick to the pan. It should be very soft and almost cuttable with a fork but still chewy.

Serve with boiled potatoes.

NOTE: This is a dish that benefits from being made ahead of time and reheated, the more often the better.

LE BOEUF MODE DE MADAME CARTET
Madame Cartet's pot roast

𝒟 𝒟 𝒟

3 pounds beef chuck
salt and pepper
1 tablespoon olive or peanut oil
lard
4 medium onions, chopped
2 cloves garlic
2 shallots, chopped
4 ounces lean bacon rind
2 tablespoons cognac or
  Calvados

1 bouquet garni (bay leaf,
  thyme, parsley)
4 tomatoes, peeled
1 pound carrots, cut into
  rounds
½ pound blanched bacon, cut
  into small pieces
2 cups rough red wine

For this recipe use beef chuck—that cut which is marbled with resinous fat and so it won't dry out during long cooking. Have your butcher roll and tie the meat for you.

Cover the meat with salt and pepper and let it marinate in your refrigerator for 24 hours. Turn from time to time.

Heat a tablespoon of olive or peanut oil and 2 tablespoons lard in a heavy casserole. Wipe the meat, then brown it on all sides over moderate heat. While it is browning, add the onions, garlic, and shallots. Be careful not to let the fat get hot enough to smoke.

Remove everything from the pot and discard the fat. Spread the bacon rind, fat side down, on the bottom of the casserole, then add the meat, onions, garlic, and shallots. Heat, then flame with the cognac or Calvados. When the flame goes out, add the bouquet garni, the carrots, the blanched bacon pieces, the peeled tomatoes, and a tablespoon of lard. Moisten with the wine.

Cover and let simmer over very low heat for 4–5 hours. Correct seasoning.

CHRISTIANE CONTICINI

Le Parc
Villemomble (Seine-Saint-Denis)

Christiane Conticini is part of that young battalion of women chefs who assure us of brilliant relief from the stuffy.

Her initiation into cooking happened long ago; the tradition was taught to her by one of the old women chefs. Gifted, intelligent, persevering, she realized quickly that culinary science, even if you have a gift, can't be learned from books. You have to get your hands into it, educate your palate.

This lovely young woman has an invincible timidity.

One has to drag confidences out of her. She is so modest she claims there is nothing interesting to say about herself.

Her work, on the other hand, she explains the way she practices it: in simple phrases and formulas such as "fresh produce, naturally and intelligently cooked, that's what cooking is. . . . *Nouvelle cuisine* isn't a break with tradition. Without those basics one could do nothing worthwhile."

The real innovation is in her use of cooking techniques. Speaking of what seems an innovation, steam cooking, she says, "One invents nothing, one rediscovers. Delicate fish, white meats, just simply salted and placed in the strainer of a couscous maker or steamer, keep all their flavor and the quality of their flesh." She has formulas such as: a sprig of mint makes all the other herbs sing. She uses lots of herbs, always with restraint.

Her husband spares her the fatigue of marketing. Several days each week he goes to Rungis. Thus they can sidestep the big deliverers and use produce chosen by themselves. herbs, vegetables from market gardens, fresh fish. He has to get up very early; by two o'clock in the morning the buyers are already numerous.

Like all creative people, Christiane doesn't repeat herself. With the same produce and the same spices she improvises, disregarding yesterday's recipe. For instance, she has stopped serving potatoes and rice and has only pasta, which she makes herself.

Her menu would fill a book on cooking. As one turns its pages, one keeps reading "in season" or "if in the market."

SAUMON CRU AUX HERBES
Raw salmon with herbs

✐ ✐ ✐

SERVES 6

This delicious hors d'oeuvre is nicest served on individual plates.

1 pound raw salmon—choose a piece from the middle of the body

4 shallots, minced

juice of 1 lemon

2 teaspoons green peppercorns, crushed

1 tablespoon minced chives

2 tablespoons minced fresh chervil, or 1 tablespoon dried

2 tablespoons mild olive oil, preferably French

1 tablespoon cognac

Peel the skin off the salmon, using a small sharp knife inserted between the skin and flesh, if necessary. Slicing parallel to the backbone, cut the flesh into thin slices. They should look like slices of smoked salmon.

Mix together the remaining ingredients (if the chervil is fresh cut it into pieces with scissors, don't chop it), then marinate the salmon in the mixture for 30 minutes in the refrigerator. Without draining the salmon, arrange it attractively on individual small plates and distribute the herbs and marinade over the pieces again, but a bit sparingly.

Serve with triangles of thin toast (as with caviar), fresh, unsalted butter, and lemon wedges.

NAVARIN DE POISSONS SUR ÉPINARDS
Poached fish on a bed of spinach

ℐℐℐ

1 sole, about 10 ounces
1 walleyed pike, about 14 ounces
½ pound shrimp or scallops
2 salmon steaks, each about ½
   inch thick, cut into thick strips
   like fat French fries
2 pounds fresh spinach

Stock

1¾ pounds white fish
  trimmings
2 carrots
1 leek

1 bouquet garni (parsley,
  thyme, bay leaf)
1 onion stuck with a clove
1 cup white wine

Ask your fish store to bone and remove the heads and tails of the sole and pike and return them to you to make the stock.

Put all the ingredients for the stock into a large kettle with 8 cups of water and let boil for 30 minutes. Toss the shrimp or scallops into the boiling liquid. Let it return to a boil, then allow to cook for another 2 minutes. Remove the shellfish with a slotted spoon and keep them warm without letting them continue to cook.

Strain the stock, return it to the stove, and bring to a simmer. Poach the fish one at a time. As they become firm, lift them out of the liquid with a slotted spoon. The salmon should be cooked last. Keep all the cooked fish warm but don't continue cooking. As they cook you can prepare the spinach. First bring a pot of salted water to a boil.

Wash the spinach and tear off and discard the stems and central veins. Drop the leaves into boiling salted water for a few minutes—just until they soften and turn an intense green. Drain.

Beurre blanc
8 ounces (2 sticks) butter
2 tablespoons minced shallots
1 cup dry white wine
3 tablespoons crème fraîche, at
    room temperature
salt and pepper

Melt 4 tablespoons butter in a saucepan and cook the shallots until they are soft but not brown. Add the wine, then boil to reduce until the liquid is almost evaporated and add a level tablespoon of crème fraîche. Stir with a wire whisk. Stirring constantly, reduce again by half, lower the heat, and then, still stirring, begin adding the rest of the butter by small pieces. Finally add the rest of the crème fraîche, pouring in a thin stream and beating constantly (as you would a mayonnaise). Whatever you do, don't let it boil. Salt and pepper to taste.

To serve, arrange a bed of spinach on heated individual plates or a heated serving platter, and cover with assorted fish and shellfish. Spoon some of the beurre blanc over the dish and serve the rest separately in a sauceboat.

NOTE: Poaching the fragile fish is easier to do if you have a kettle with a removable strainer or if you lower it in a frying basket or, at the most primitive, in a sieve. Best of all, of course, is a fish poacher.

LOTTE À LA RHUBARBE
Bellyfish with rhubarb

🖋 🖋 🖋

6 pieces bellyfish (or any firm-
    fleshed fish such as cod, whiting,
    or halibut), weighing about
    4 pounds all together

Fumet

1½ pounds trimmings from
    white fish
2 carrots
2 leeks
1 bouquet garni (thyme,
    parsley, bay leaf)

1 onion stuck with a clove
3 stalks celery
salt and pepper
1 bottle dry white wine

Rhubarb purée

2–2½ pounds rhubarb (weighed
    without leaves)
4 ounces (1 stick) butter
½ cup crème fraîche
salt and pepper

Sauce

6 ounces (1½ sticks) butter
2 tablespoons minced shallots
2 tablespoons heavy cream, at
    room temperature
1 lemon

Fumet

Put all the ingredients for the fumet in a large kettle with ⅓ wine to ⅔ water (6 cups and 12 cups is a good amount for this dish). Let boil for 30 minutes, then turn off the heat and let the stock cool. When it is tepid, strain and return to the kettle.

Poach the pieces of fish in the stock. Bring it to the threshold of a boil and let it cook without quite bubbling for 5 minutes. Turn off the heat and keep the fish warm in the stock.

Rhubarb purée

Cut the rhubarb stalks into slices about ½ inch long. Toss them into boiling salted water and cook for about 5 minutes or until they are soft. Remove the rhubarb and drain. Melt the butter, then put it, with the poached stems, into a blender or food processor or purée through a food mill or sieve. Add the crème fraîche and salt and pepper. If the purée is too liquid put it over moderate heat and let the liquid evaporate. It should be about the consistency, although not the texture, of applesauce.

Sauce

Melt 3 tablespoons of the butter and add the minced shallots. Cook without letting them brown until they are a paste. Add 2 cups fish fumet and reduce over high heat to about half. Add a teaspoon of cream and reduce some more, then add the remaining butter a spoonful at a time, stirring constantly with a wire whisk and amalgamating each piece before you add the next. Squirt in lemon juice from time to time as you stir in the butter. Add the rest of the cream, beating constantly to incorporate it. Do not let the sauce boil again after you have added the last of the cream. Correct seasoning.

Reheat all parts of this dish. Arrange the drained fish on a serving platter and spoon some sauce over it. Pass the rest in a sauceboat and serve the purée separately. Serve on hot plates.

The rhubarb purée is not a vegetable side dish—it is more like a surprising condiment for the fish.

NOTES : Bellyfish is a fish with a large central bone and no little bones, so when the recipe calls for 6 pieces it means three slices from the midsection, which will divide neatly into 6 serving pieces.

The rhubarb purée can be made well ahead and reheated, and the shallots can be cooked in the butter and then in the fumet for the sauce ahead of time, too. You can be doing these steps while the fumet is cooking and finish the sauce while the fish cooks.

BLANQUETTE DE VOLAILLE AUX PETITS RADIS
Light chicken stew with tiny radishes

❧ ❧ ❧

The chicken is cooked in the steam from a very fragrant stock, which then becomes the basis for the sauce.

> 1 roasting chicken, about 3½–4
>   pounds
> salt and pepper
> 2 bunches (about 40) radishes,
>   preferably white, as the red
>   lose their color when cooked
> about 40 tiny white onions
> 6 ounces small mushrooms

Stock

the chicken carcass	1 turnip
3 carrots	salt and pepper
3 onions	1 clove
4 stalks celery	1 bouquet garni (parsley,
3 leeks	thyme, 1 bay leaf)

Sauce

reduced stock	1 lemon
8 ounces (2 sticks) butter, soft-	2 tablespoons chopped fresh
ened at room temperature	chervil, or 1 teaspoon dried
3 tablespoons heavy cream	

Cut the raw chicken as you would carve a cooked bird. Cut off the wings and the legs with the second joints and then slice off the breast meat. If the breast fillets are particularly large divide them. Salt and pepper the meat and set it aside in the refrigerator.

Stock

Choose a pot your colander will fit on top of tightly or use a regular steamer to make this stock. In the pot (without the colander or steamer) place the carcass, the wing tips, and the gizzard of the chicken. Coarsely chop the vegetables, add them to the pot along with seasonings, and pour in water to cover. Cook for about $1\frac{1}{2}$ hours or until the vegetables and chicken parts have cooked into a fine fragrant broth. Strain the broth and set aside $2\frac{1}{2}$ cups in another pot to make the sauce. Return the rest of the bouillon to the stock pot.

Arrange the pieces of raw chicken in an even layer on the bottom of a colander or steamer and place over the bouillon. The colander should fit tightly so that the steam passes through the holes in the colander rather than up the sides. If there are big gaps at the sides, wrap with aluminum foil. Put a cover over the colander. Chicken prepared this way will cook more rapidly than you would think, depending on the size of the bird.

Check after 45 minutes.

While the chicken is cooking, bring salted water to a simmer and cook the radishes and onions together. When the point of a knife pierces them easily they are cooked. Add the mushrooms to the water and turn off the heat under the pot. Let the vegetables cool, rather than keeping them hot, which would make them overcook.

Also while the chicken is cooking, bring the reserved 2½ cups of strained stock to a rapid boil and reduce it to 4 tablespoons. Let it cool to tepid.

When the chicken is done turn off the heat under the pot and keep the chicken warm in the colander with the mushrooms, onions, and radishes.

Sauce

Heat the cream to body temperature in a double boiler and have the butter at room temperature. Add 1 tablespoon of the cream to the reduced stock and boil down some more until it coats a wooden spoon. Cut the soft butter into pieces the size of a small nut and add two or three pieces at a time over low heat, stirring well after each addition to dissolve it completely.

As you stir in the butter, from time to time squeeze in a little lemon juice. When all the butter is added and the sauce is the consistency of a thick mayonnaise, beat in the warm cream in a steady stream. Keep beating until it is all incorporated. Off the heat correct the seasoning and add the chervil.

Spoon over the chicken and the vegetables on a heated serving platter.

POT-AU-FEU EN GELÉE
Beef and vegetables in aspic

S S S

SERVES 6

2 pounds boned short ribs

1¼ pounds chuck or top or
bottom round beef, as you
prefer

1 pound cracked veal knuckle

5 leeks

1 small head celery separated
into stalks, rinsed and peeled
to remove its strings

8 carrots

5 turnips

2 onions

4 cloves

salt and peppercorns

tarragon leaves

about 1 teaspoon chervil

about 1 teaspoon chives

Bring 4 quarts of water to a boil and add the meat and bones.
Let cook for 2½ hours at a very low boil, really a simmer.
Skim.

Add the vegetables: tie the leeks into a bundle and the
celery stalks into another. The carrots, turnips, and onions
can go in as is. Add the cloves, salt, and 10 peppercorns, and
cook for 3–4 hours over very low heat.

Remove the meat and vegetables from the stock and discard the bones. Slice the meat into smallish flat pieces (between the size of a quarter and a fifty-cent piece) and peel
all the vegetables, then slice them into rounds no bigger than
the pieces of meat. In a large terrine or deep, square dish
arrange a judicious assortment of a third of the vegetables.
Scatter several tarragon leaves over them, then top with half
the meat slices placed to make a flat bed. Scatter more tarragon.

Alternate layers of meat and vegetables with a few tarragon leaves between each, and end with the last third of the vegetables. Press gently to tamp down. Let cool completely.

Degrease the cooking stock and reduce to about 4 cups, then let cool. Chop the chervil and the chives finely and when the liquid is half cold stir them in, then pour over the cold terrine. Poke a knife around to the bottom of the dish in several places so the liquid penetrates the whole dish. Do this several times until the aspic has jelled. If there is bouillon left over (and there should be) chill and jell it, too, to serve, cubed, with the terrine. Refrigerate this dish for 8 hours before serving.

NOTES: It is very easy to degrease stock if you let it chill first. The fat rises to the top and congeals and you can just skim it off.

This aspic can be made with gelatin instead of veal knuckles. If you want to do it this way, cook according to directions until the point when you reduce the stock to about 4 cups. Then dissolve 2 envelopes of gelatin in a little cold water and stir into the hot stock. The rest of the directions remain the same.

SOUPE AUX FRUITS
Fruit soup

This is an astonishing dessert—an orange juice custard holds prunes, grapefruit sections, strawberries, and raspberries, served hot in individual glasses.

6 sweet oranges	6 egg yolks
2 grapefruits	extra-fine sugar
12–15 prunes, preferably pitted	orange liqueur, your choice:
1 quart strawberries	Grand Marnier, Cointreau,
1 pint raspberries	Marasquin

Squeeze the oranges. They should yield about 2 cups of juice. Peel the grapefruits, divide them into sections, and remove all skin on the sections. Soak the prunes in tepid water to cover for several hours. Take the stems off the strawberries and halve them if they are large.

Heat the orange juice over low heat until it begins to quiver, then add the skinned grapefruit sections, the drained, inflated prunes, and the strawberries.

Just before the juice reaches the boil, remove the fruits with a slotted spoon and let them cool.

Beat the egg yolks with 4 tablespoons sugar until they lighten and thicken. Reheat the juice (add any juice that has drained off the cooling fruits, too), and, stirring constantly, pour into the beaten yolks. Return to the heat and continue to stir until the mixture thickens like a custard and coats a wooden spoon. Taste and add more sugar to your taste and the liqueur of your choice.

To serve divide the cooked fruits and the raspberries among individual stemmed glasses and cover with the hot sauce.

You may serve this dessert at room temperature but not chilled.

GISÈLE CROUZIER

La Croix Blanche
Chaumont-sur-Tharonne
(Loir-et-Cher)

At Gisèle Crouzier's, as soon as you enter you are aware of the spirit of the place. That is because one must go through the kitchen to get to the dining room.

And what a kitchen!—chocolate-caramel-colored with its beautiful posters, as brilliant as a pure silk dress, and its canisters and copper pots all sparkling. You rush to inhale the secrets of the covered pots on the "piano." That's what they call the giant stoves where these great women chefs play their scales. Their symphonies, I should say.

Gisèle Crouzier is from Périgord—all her menus proclaim that. A teacher, recycled as a chef, she has exchanged her enthusiasm for the multiplication tables for dining tables.

Having lived for many years in this more than five-hundred-year-old inn in Sologne, a countryside rich in game and fish-stocked ponds, she has mastered truffles and foie gras, preserved goose and duck, the science of savory terrines, nut oil, and the famous *mique*, a rustic brioche cooked in a bouillon.

From the *mique* one passes to the brioche, the real thing —soft, buttery. It is the finial of desserts, which here dazzle in their abundance.

LAPIN ALBICOCO
Rabbit fricassee

✑✑✑

This is a rabbit fricassee curiously garnished with cooked dried apricots and sweetened with apricot preserves.

1 young rabbit, 2½–3 pounds

Marinade
1 bottle dry white wine
1 large or 2 medium onions,
   sliced
2 shallots, minced
1 small bunch parsley, chopped

Cut the rabbit into serving pieces. The anatomy is unfamiliar, and you will find that the most natural way to divide the animal is into two pieces for each hind leg, one for each side of the breast, and four for the saddle and forelegs—a piece for the ribs on each side and one each for the front legs.

Mix all ingredients for the marinade together and pour over the rabbit. The meat should be covered. Let marinate for 24–48 hours in a cool place or in the refrigerator, turning two or three times.

Cooking
1 tablespoon butter
2 tablespoons olive oil
2 medium carrots, diced
1 turnip, diced
1 leek, white part only, diced

1 medium onion, diced
1 clove garlic, minced
salt and pepper
1 tablespoon apricot preserves

Strain the marinade through a colander and reserve the liquid and the solids. Pat the rabbit meat dry, then brown it and the vegetables from the marinade in a casserole in a little butter or oil, being careful not to burn the fat.

In another pan heat a tablespoon of olive oil and brown —one vegetable at a time—the carrots, the turnip, the leek, the onion, and the garlic. Bring the marinating liquid to a boil and let cook for 10 minutes. Combine all the separately browned vegetables in the hot marinade and pour everything over the pieces of rabbit in the casserole. Add salt and pepper and the apricot preserves.

Bring to a gentle boil so the meat doesn't fall apart. While it cooks, prepare the apricots (see below). When the rabbit is cooked, which should be in 45 minutes to 1½ hours depending on the size of the rabbit (you should be able to pierce the flesh easily), remove it from the liquid and keep warm. Strain the sauce and press on the vegetables in the sieve to extract all their juices. Correct the seasoning and return the rabbit to the hot sauce.

Arrange the pieces of rabbit on a serving platter and spoon the sauce over them. Surround the meat with the cooked apricots.

Apricots
½ pound dried apricots
6–8 sugar lumps
2 tablespoons aprciot preserves

Wash the apricots and place them in a saucepan with the sugar, the preserves, and enough water to cover well. Bring to a boil over a 3-minute period, then cover and reduce the heat to very low and let the apricots inflate for 30 minutes. Do not let them boil or even simmer. If they are too juicy, remove them from the liquid and reduce the syrup at a high boil.

MIQUE ROYALE AUX ROGNONS DE VEAU AUX MORILLES
Brioche with veal kidneys and morels

↗↗↗

SERVES 6

A *mique* is a rustic brioche from the Sarlat region, cooked in a bouillon. As with all raised-dough breads, it should be made the day before it is to be used, so it becomes a bit stale.

Dough

1 package yeast
3½ cups flour
6 eggs
large pinch salt

1 teaspoon sugar
4 ounces (1 stick) butter, softened

about 6 cups beef or chicken stock

Dissolve the yeast in ½ cup of warm water, then mix in enough of the flour to make a soft but not too liquid ball of dough. Place in a large bowl, cover with a towel, and set aside in a warm place. It should double in volume. This is your yeast sponge.

In a bowl of an electric mixer (with a dough hook if you have one) put the rest of the flour, the eggs, salt, and sugar. Mix well, then, bit by bit, beat in the yeast sponge, and finally the softened butter. Beat until the dough pulls away from the beaters and the sides of the bowl.

Turn the dough out onto a piece of muslin or a tea towel and tie it up loosely like a hobo's bundle, but don't leave any holes. There should be enough room for the dough to double in volume as it rises, but not escape as it cooks.

In a large round or oval casserole bring stock to a boil. It can be beef or chicken stock—it doesn't matter so long as it has a good perfume. Plunge the dough-filled package into the boiling stock (the stock must cover the dough) and cook for about 20 minutes. Test with a long needle or skewer. If it comes out clean the *mique* is cooked.

Remove it from the bouillon and place on a rack. Unwrap the muslin. You should have a round or oval thick loaf.

The morels

2 ounces dried morels, or fresh
   if available
1 tablespoon butter
5–6 shallots, minced
¾ cup heavy cream
salt and pepper

Wash the morels quickly in lots of water to rid them of any sand that might still be clinging to them. Let them inflate for 20 minutes in a little warm water. Drain them.

Melt the butter in a saucepan and cook the shallots until they are soft, but don't let them brown. When they are ready, add the cream and the morels. Cook 5–8 minutes. Add salt and pepper and set aside.

The kidneys

3 large veal kidneys
2 ounces (½ stick) butter

Trim the fat off the kidneys and cut them into pieces the size of small walnuts.

In a frying pan soften half the butter over low heat, then add the kidneys and cook just to stiffen. Don't let them brown. Add the contents of the morel pan and cook them together. The kidneys should remain somewhat bloody on the inside. If they are cooked longer than about 5 minutes they lose their savor and harden. Correct seasoning.

Cut the *mique* into slices the thickness of a zwieback and fry the slices in the remaining butter. Remove the kidneys from the pot with a slotted spoon and arrange them on the slices of fried bread on a platter. Spoon the sauce over them at the last minute and serve hot.

TARTE SOLOGNOTE AUX POIRES
Pear tart

ﻬ ﻬ ﻬ

The pastry

1½ cups flour

4 tablespoons cornstarch

½ cup sugar

5 eggs

6 tablespoons crème fraîche

2 tablespoons pear-flavored
eau-de-vie

Sift the flour and cornstarch together into a bowl. Add the other ingredients, mixing well. Set aside in the refrigerator. This will make a heavy, custardy liquid, not like a usual pastry dough at all.

Preheat oven to 350°F. before you begin the next step.

The pears

2 ounces (½ stick) butter

1 cup extra-fine sugar

5 medium pears (ripe but firm)

Butter the pan, using all the butter. Sprinkle the bottom as evenly as possible with the extra-fine sugar.

Peel the pears, halve them, and remove the pits and cores. Arrange them attractively and symmetrically on the sugar, rounded side down.

Place the pan over fairly low heat, regulating it so that the sugar will caramelize and turn golden but won't get too dark or burn. This will be easier if you straddle the pan over the edges of two burners rather than centering it on one. On one burner the center tends to burn and the edges never caramelize.

When the sugar has caramelized, immediately cover the pears with the prepared pastry, pouring and spreading it as evenly as you can, and pop into the preheated oven.

When the pastry is firm and the sides pull away from the pan (20–25 minutes), remove the tart from the oven. Unmold the tart upside down onto a heated serving dish. If the tart cools off return it to the oven and serve it warm or rewarmed.

GÂTEAU AUX NOIX
Nut cake

𝒮𝒮𝒮

Pâte sucrée

1¾ cups flour

4 ounces (1 stick) butter,
   softened

½ cup extra-fine sugar

1 teaspoon vanilla sugar

1 pinch salt

1 egg

Measure the flour, then sift it onto a counter or tabletop. Using your fingertips, blend in the softened butter until the consistency is fairly uniform, then wrap in waxed paper and set aside for 2 hours in the refrigerator.

Turn the mixture out onto the counter or tabletop again and make a well in the center. Into the well put the two sugars, the salt, and the egg. Mix very rapidly with your hands, then *fraisez* the dough: that means to push a little bit away from you across the surface of the table or counter, using the heel of your hand. Break all of the dough, then reassemble into a ball and break it all again, but no more than twice. This should make it very homogeneous. Re-form into a ball and set aside in a cool place or the refrigerator for 2 more hours.

Butter and flour the cake pan, then turn it over and tap out any excess flour. If the dough has been in the refrigerator, you may have to let it come to room temperature before you can roll it. When it is malleable, roll to about ½-inch thickness, then roll it around your rolling pin (it will be very fragile) and lay it over the top of the prepared cake pan.

Press it into place with your fingertips and let it come up beyond the rim of the pan in a crest about ½ inch high. Bracing the outside of the crest with your fingers, mark the inside obliquely with the back of the tines of a fork. Set aside in the refrigerator.

Nut filling

4 ounces (½ cup) chopped nuts (see note)

½ cup sugar

1 teaspoon vanilla sugar

1 tablespoon kirsch

1 tablespoon orange liqueur, preferably Marasquin

1 tablespoon honey

2 eggs, separated

2 tablespoons cornstarch or potato starch

2 ounces butter, melted

Preheat oven to 375°F.

Mix together the first six filling ingredients in the order listed, then beat in the egg yolks.

Beat with a wooden spoon or an electric beater until the mixture is light-colored, then add the starch and the melted butter.

Beat the whites into soft peaks, then stir ¼ cup or so of the whites into the nut mixture to lighten it. Now fold the rest of the whites into the nut mixture, being careful to lift up the heavier mass from the bottom as you fold.

Turn the mixture into the prepared crust, smooth the top, and put into the preheated oven.

After 15 minutes check the cake and if it is browning too rapidly put a piece of waxed paper over the top. Pay particular attention to the edges of the crust. The cake should be done in 30 minutes—look to see that the center is firm: if you put a toothpick into it, it will come out clean.

79

NOTES: You may use any kind of nuts, but blanched almonds, with their affinity for honey, are particularly good in this recipe.

In an 8-by-2-inch pan the filling will come only about halfway up the crust walls. If you prefer a fuller crust use a 9-by-1-inch pan, but then cut the cooking time by about 5–7 minutes.

GEORGETTE DESCAT

Lous Landès
Paris 14ᵉ

Blonde, like good butter, cropped like a young recruit, rosy from never backing away from her stove, open, lively, generous—that is how Georgette Descat, one of the doyennes of the great women chefs, appears in her minuscule kitchen.

She speaks picturesquely, with lots of life and a bit of irony.

"*La nouvelle cuisine!* but that's the way I've always done things. Vegetables still firm, just right; fish pink at the bone; liaisons without flour—good farm butter is enough. But top-quality products from good places. Each dish made at the moment, not waiting in the refrigerator and reheated. Come, you'll see."

A very small kitchen with the central "piano" of restaurant cooking. There's enough room for Georgette to stretch out her arms to open the refrigerator, to lift them to unhook a pot. She doesn't go miles, but stays in place, squeezed between her helpers, surrounded by lots of nervous tension, which leaves her exhausted and happy. It's her life and she loves what she does.

"When I was a child I cooked; cooking was going on all around the house. We weren't rich but we ate like princes. We bought skinny, young chickens and fattened them. Often during the war they served as barter to dress my children: two boys, one girl. They all know how to cook. My daughter worked with me for several years, then she and her husband left to start their own place in Gastes. The older boy, whom you see over there, is my surrogate in contacts with guests and tradespeople. He has an experienced palate that knows how to choose wines. The other, in Pau, has an insurance company. It remains to be seen how he cooks.

"You will be surprised to learn that I sell my foie gras, my preserves, and my cassoulets retail even in midsummer. Nowadays one can find fresh duck foie gras all year round. My preparations know no season.

"Game, on the other hand, does have its season. In my territory, landes [a kind of game bird], like the one shown on my sign, have become rare. Doves, ortolans, woodcocks— their prices have gotten almost prohibitive. But it's justified by their quality: they're really wild, not domestic.

"Ortolans are little migratory birds and you catch them with a net. Then you put them into a cage with lots of food and the seeds of all the field grasses. Gluttons, with nothing to do, they eat all day and all night (you leave a light on full time to fool them). In twenty days they are as fat as you could wish.

"I cook them in little packets. Each ortolan is salted, peppered, and then wrapped in aluminum foil and put into a very hot oven for four or five minutes. Our ovens are very powerful—in a home oven it would take maybe a few minutes more. . . . The packets are served as they come out of the oven. There are some gourmets who hide under their napkins to eat ortolans so they can suck on them and not lose any of the juice. My dishes with foie gras, with cèpes, with truffles, are my invention. Anyone can make them. They are good as a first course or a one-dish meal. And my noodles are fresh, made by me. And my cèpes and truffles are put up by me.

"*Magret* means 'little thin thing.' It is a duck breast fillet. Some years ago I was the only one serving them. Now they're popular. The skin is peeled off, then the fillet is sautéed in duck fat in a frying pan so it's golden on both sides. Then you cover the pan for a few minutes so the meat can swell. It is served like a steak, rare, medium, or whatever, and accompanied by potatoes also sautéed in goose or duck fat.

"The rest of the duck is preserved. I always have some on the stove. To think, I use two hundred each month."

Watching Georgette work is also a lesson in organization. In a few minutes, before my eyes, she cooked a fish stew for four. It's true the stock had already been prepared and stored in big crocks in the refrigerator. There it is, ready to poach shellfish, salt-water fish, and those from fresh waters—such as that slice of stuffed pike simmering in its own pot.

At the same time coming from the oven were the fumes of a whole duck liver for three people which would be served sliced and in its own juices, then sprinkled with minced truffles, wrapped in a piece of aluminum foil, and reheated in stock waiting on the back of the stove. I learned many things at Georgette Descat's.

NOUILLES FRAÎCHES DE GEORGETTE
Georgette's fresh noodles

∅∅∅

This recipe assumes you will be using a pasta machine. It could be done by hand but would be extremely tedious.

> 3 cups flour
> 4 eggs
> 1 tablespoon olive oil
> 2 tablespoons water
> salt

Knead all the ingredients together to mix them, then roll the dough out in a pasta machine. Roll a small piece first several times through the widest setting of the rollers (number 8), then, narrowing the gap one notch at a time, run the dough through, making it thinner and thinner. After going through number 3 it should be perfect—supple as satin.

Cut into noodles about ½ inch wide, and as soon as they are cut drape them over a broomstick. Repeat with the rest of the dough. They have to dry so that their surface will weather and they will stretch out. This should take about 6–8 hours. Then gather the dried noodles into loose clusters, like big skeins of yarn, and let them air on a dishcloth for 24 hours.

When you cook them, cook them *al dente*—until still firm to the bite—in lots of lightly salted water containing 1 tablespoon of olive oil. Drained, the noodles can be stored, ready to use, in a corked crock in the refrigerator for several days.

NOUILLES AU FOIE GRAS
Noodles with foie gras

✐ ✐ ✐

2 tablespoons fresh, dried, or preserved cèpes (see following recipe)

2 ounces fresh foie gras (see note)

3 tablespoons goose fat or 2 tablespoons olive oil

2 ounces raw fresh noodles

salt and crushed pepper

⅛ ounce fresh truffles, cut into a matchstick julienne

If cèpes are dried, soak them until inflated.

Bring a large pot of salted water to a boil.

Slice the foie gras into pieces about the same thickness as the cèpes (approximately ½ inch). Heat the goose fat or oil in a large skillet. Drop the noodles into the boiling water and the foie gras and cèpes into the hot fat.

The foie gras and cèpes will have cooked enough in a few minutes. Add the cooked, perfectly drained noodles to the skillet, then add salt and crushed pepper.

Using two forks, lift the mass and turn it over and over to reheat the noodles and coat them with sauce. Add the truffles and serve at once.

N O T E S : If you use commercial pasta for this dish use very thin linguine and cook it before starting on the foie gras. You can undercook it and leave it in the water, then drain it and add to the skillet at the last minute, or drain it and coat it with a little oil so it doesn't clump.

Despite the expense, truffles really are a wonderful part of this dish. You can, of course, use preserved ones.

You can also substitute canned foie gras or pâté de foie gras for the fresh.

CÈPES EN CONSERVE
Preserved cèpes

𝒯 𝒯 𝒯

very fresh cèpes
peanut oil

Wipe, don't wash, the mushrooms, then lightly scrape any stems which might have broken off the caps. Don't peel any skin off unless you can't remove some earth. Slice those stems the long way about ¼ inch wide.

If there are any loose caps without stems, dice them finely. Then cook everything in pure peanut oil to cover, hot enough so it bubbles up but doesn't boil over when the mushrooms are put into it. Once they are in, raise the heat to high and stir often.

Cooking time is short. The mushrooms are ready when the flesh is still slightly crunchy to the teeth but soft on the inside.

Remove the mushrooms at once to sterilized canning jars. Cover them with their cooking oil and when they are cold, seal the jars.

If you plan to use the mushrooms within 3 or 4 weeks they will keep perfectly well in the refrigerator. But if you would like to save them for a year they must be preserved by either heating or freezing.

To preserve by heat use a pressure cooker and cook for 2 hours in jars as though you were canning.

If you prefer to freeze them, pour them into special

sealable plastic bags and freeze. When you want to use them, don't thaw them but remove in frozen blocks from the bag and drop into peanut oil heated in a large preserving kettle so the oil won't spatter so much when the cold block is dropped in. Cook until the mushrooms are the right temperature and consistency.

LE POT-AU-FEU DE POISSON DE GEORGETTE
Georgette's fish stew

ⅅ ⅅ ⅅ

Fumet for fish stew

2 large leeks

2 carrots

2 turnips

2 onions

6 cloves garlic

1 head celery

1 bouquet garni (parsley,
    thyme, ¼ bay leaf)

3 pounds white fish scraps
    (head and back of sole, trout,
    whiting, etc.)

1 tablespoon olive oil

3 tomatoes, peeled, seeded, and
    finely diced

Bring 12 cups of water to a boil with the green parts of the leeks (save the whites), the carrots, turnips, 1 onion, and 3 cloves of the garlic. Cut off and reserve 5 inches at the base of the celery, then tie the stalks together with the bouquet garni and add them, too.

Bring to a boil, and after it has boiled for 10–15 minutes add the fish scraps. Cover and cook at a low boil for about 30 minutes. Let cool, then strain, but don't press on the solid residue in the sieve. You should have about 8 cups of stock.

Put half (4 cups) in a saucepan over moderate heat and boil down to a little more than half.

While it is reducing, mince the white of the leeks, the remaining onion, 3 cloves garlic, and the celery base with strings removed. Heat the olive oil in a skillet and over low heat cook the minced vegetables, stirring often, until they are soft. Don't let them take color.

Have the tomatoes ready. You are going to add them to the skillet when the vegetables are soft and then you will turn the contents of the skillet into the reduced stock.

The fish

8 langoustines or 1 pound shrimp	4 squid, coarsely cut up
	1½ pounds mussels
4 pieces bellyfish or any firm-fleshed fish such as cod, halibut, or striped bass	½ pound small green beans
	4 carrots
4 fillets of walleyed pike	2 turnips
½ pound scallops	2–3 potatoes
	olive oil

Julienne the carrots and turnips and cut the potatoes into a large dice. Cook the beans in salted, boiling water until they are done but still crunchy, then drain and set them aside. Cook the other vegetables in concentrated fish stock at a bare simmer until they too are cooked but still crunchy. Turn off the heat and let them sit in the stock.

Heat the fumet to cook the fish just to a bare quiver. Have the fish ready near the stove and add them in order: langoustines or shrimp and bellyfish first, then 5 minutes later the pike and scallops. Meanwhile heat some olive oil in a skillet and cook the squid pieces quickly, then add the mussels. When they open, turn the contents of the skillet into the fish kettle.

To arrange in the serving bowl first place the pieces of fish and shellfish so they don't overlap, then sprinkle the beans and the other cooked vegetables around them.

To the stock in which the fish were cooked add 3 spoonfuls of the reduced fumet. Bring to a boil and pour, boiling, over the bowl of fish.

POT-AU-FEU AUX QUATRE VIANDES

Pot-au-feu with four meats

𝒮 𝒮 𝒮

SERVES 8

This pot-au-feu is perfect for a one-dish meal. It can be prepared and cooked the day before it is to be served.

1 veal breast, about 3 pounds,
with a pocket for stuffing

Stuffing

10 ounces bacon

1 pound boned pork (any firm cut: shoulder, blade, loin)

7 ounces ham

5–6 ounces trimmings from the breast of veal (or equivalent weight in boned chicken)

2 medium onions

2 cloves garlic

3 slices toast, or ½–⅔ cup bread crumbs

2–3 eggs

pepper

Meats

2½ pounds chuck pot roast or boned short ribs

2½ pounds blade or shoulder or half a pork butt, bone in

2½-pound roasting chicken

Vegetables

4 fine leeks

1 medium cabbage

1 pound carrots, peeled

1 head celery, in stalks, stringed

1 pound small turnips, peeled

1 cucumber

Cut the leeks in half where the white changes to green. Tie the green into bundles and put them, with the beef, into 17 cups cold water. Bring to a boil. Skim. Let cook at a gentle boil for 1½ hours.

While the beef cooks, blanch the head of cabbage in a large pot of boiling water for about 5 minutes, then drain, remove, and set aside the largest outer leaves, and quarter the head, removing the core.

Stuff the breast of veal.

Remove any skin or bones from all the stuffing meats, then put all the stuffing ingredients except the eggs and the pepper into a meat grinder or food processor. When they are ground, knead the pepper and two of the eggs into the mixture. Don't add the third egg unless it is too thick—it should be about the consistency of mashed potatoes, but obviously not the same texture. Wrap in one layer of the blanched large, outer cabbage leaves.

Stuff this bundle into the pocket in the veal breast. It shouldn't stretch too much or it might burst when cooking. Sew the openings closed with a trussing needle and thread.

When the beef has cooked for 1½ hours add the stuffed breast and the pork. Return to a boil and simmer another 1½ hours—as gently as possible.

While this round of cooking is going on, prepare the vegetables. Tie the whites of the leeks into bundles so they don't break apart—you will cut the string to serve. Quarter the carrots, the long way, then slice the stringed celery stalks into 3-inch pieces, and tie them into bundles, too. When the meat has cooked its 1½ hours, add these vegetables plus the whole (if small) turnips and the cucumber, unpeeled but cut in half, and finally the blanched cabbage quarters. When they have all boiled for 15 minutes, remove from the heat and let cool, uncovered.

The next day, to serve, first degrease the surface of the stock. Then remove the meats and the veal breast and the vegetables. Discard the leek greens. Put the chicken into the stock and reheat over medium heat. When it comes to a boil let the chicken cook for 20 minutes, then remove it from the stock, carve it, and keep it warm.

While the stock is reheating and the chicken is cooking, cut the cold meats into serving pieces, then reassemble them and wrap them in aluminum foil. When you have removed the chicken, return the wrapped meats and the vegetables to the hot stock for about 5 minutes or until they are reheated. Taste and salt if necessary. Arrange the meats on a serving platter and just before you are about to serve give each person a cup of the bouillon poured through a dampened, wrung-out tea towel folded in four to degrease thoroughly.

If you want to serve boiled potatoes with this dinner, cook them separately.

NOTES: You will probably have to cook this in two large pots unless you have a restaurant-sized kettle. Cook the leek and beef stock first, then when it is ready divide it into two large pots, add the meats—some to one pot, some to the other—then pour in more water to cover.

When you slice the cold meats and wrap them in aluminum foil prior to the last reheating you might find it easier to retrieve them if you tie them up with white string. Wrap in the foil, then enfold in clean tea towels to keep the package compact (this will probably be necessary only for the stuffed breast, because the stuffing is loose), then put a piece of string around each bundle of foil or towel, the way you would a package to be mailed. That way, when you are trying to get the meat out of the hot stock you can catch hold of the string to pull it out.

ANNIE DESVIGNES

La Tour du Roy
Vervins-en-Thiérache (Aisne)

Annie Desvignes is one of the Lequy sisters of the Auberge Fleurise in Sars-Poterie.

Already supplied with a little bundle of culinary knowledge, she had the wisdom to find her masters: Lenotre for patisserie, Raymond Oliver, and Claude Peyrot of Vivarois for cooking. This before opening her own place five years ago.

Helped by her young husband, who was just out of hotel school, polished in the best restaurants in France—it still took a big dose of courage and all the audacity of youth to attempt this undertaking.

La Tour du Roy, which was a manor house flanked by the towers that give it its name, rich in historical memories but almost in ruins, has become a modern country inn.

Everything is cooked when it is ordered except dishes that are simmered in the old way—such as rabbit with cider as the Thiérache peasants cook it or hare *à l'ancienne*.

Annie's sauces rise on butter: that is, they are bound without flour, shored up on the subtle flavor of reduced juices from the food being cooked—really flavored creams.

The resources of Annie's region are perhaps not too diversified, but grazing land gives the meat and milk products a discernable flavor, astonishing in good crème fraîche taken from the farm and generously served in soup bowls with her famous desserts. Her apple tart à la Duflot, exquisite because of the quality of her pastry and the flavor of her apples, is a rare delight.

In the wine cellar one must cite the cider, served cold in champagne bottles. But the proprietor, who has collected a large and fine cellar from the best vineyards, doesn't let your choice stop there. He has other things to suggest to you, the better to help you appreciate his wife's "useful works."

TURBOTIN À L'OSEILLE
Flounder with sorrel

✐ ✐ ✐

1 flounder, about 4½ pounds
3 tablespoons butter
5–6 ounces sorrel, chopped
⅔ cup crème fraîche
salt and pepper

For cooking the fish
4 cups milk
1½ teaspoons coarse salt

Scald the milk and let cool.

Ask your fish store to detach the fillets of the flounder (the skin won't come off).

Begin with the sauce. Melt the butter in a small pot and add the chopped sorrel, turning it over and over so it wilts quickly. As soon as it is wilted, without letting it cook any more, add the crème fraîche and reduce it, stirring constantly, until it coats a wooden spoon. Add salt and pepper.

In a large shallow pan such as a *sautoir* heat the scalded milk with the coarse salt until it feels warm to your fingers, but you can stand to put them in. Stretch the fillets out in the milk and continue to cook. When the black skin comes off with no trouble the cooking is finished. Arrange the fish on a serving plate and spoon the very hot sauce over them.

Annie Desvignes goes over the finished dish with a salamander (a portable broiler) to brown the surface of the sauce and reheat the whole dish. You can run the dish under the broiler for a moment.

FILETS DE DORADE AUX PETITS LÉGUMES
Fillets of porgy with vegetables

✑✑✑

SERVES 8

4 porgies, 1½–2 pounds each,
   filleted
salt and pepper
2 cups fish stock (see below)
4 leeks, whites only
4 medium carrots
4 ounces lettuce

4 ounces (1 stick) butter
4 shallots
4 ounces mushrooms, chopped
2 cups tomato sauce (see
   below)
2 tablespoons heavy cream
flour (optional)

Fish stock
1–1¼ pounds white fish
   trimmings
1 onion
1 large clove garlic
1 carrot
1 bouquet garni (bay leaf,
   thyme, parsley)

Tomato sauce
4 tablespoons olive oil
2 small onions, roughly
   chopped
1 clove garlic
1 bouquet garni (thyme, bay
   leaf, parsley, tarragon)

2 pounds ripe tomatoes,
   quartered
salt and pepper

99

Stock

Put all the ingredients for the stock into a large kettle with about 4 cups of water. Boil for 25 minutes. Strain and press on the solids left in the bottom of the sieve to extract all their juices, then discard. Set the stock aside.

Tomato sauce

In a heavy-bottom saucepan heat the oil, then add the onions, the whole peeled clove of garlic, and the bouquet garni. Cook over moderate heat until the onions are soft, but don't let them take on color.

Raise the heat and add the tomatoes. Cook over high heat for several minutes, then, when they are beginning to melt down, lower the heat and let simmer until the mixture becomes a paste. Remove the bouquet garni and put the mixture through a vegetable mill or purée in a food processor and then strain. Add salt and pepper. You should have a thick but runny sauce, about the consistency of tomato juice.

Cooking the fish

Remove the skin and any forgotten bones from the fish fillets and arrange them on an ovenproof platter (a gratin dish is perfect for this). Salt and pepper them. Cover them with stock and put in the oven heated to the highest temperature setting.

When the stock is about to boil, turn off heat, cover the plate, and let it wait outside the oven so you don't prolong the cooking.

Sauce

Cut the leeks into thin lengthwise strips. Julienne the carrots into pieces about the same size. Blanch the lettuce for about 1 minute in boiling water.

In a heavy-bottomed pot melt half the butter (4 table-spoons). Add the leeks, carrots, and lettuce. In a few minutes all the vegetables will be tender and softened. Separate the lettuce from the leek and carrots, and set the vegetables aside.

Melt 2 tablespoons of butter in a large pot and soften the shallots, but don't let them brown. When they are soft add the chopped mushrooms and the tomato sauce. Let simmer gently.

Very carefully remove the fillets from the stock and keep them warm. Then reduce the stock to about 1 cup. Pour it into the tomato sauce and let simmer again while you arrange your service plate. Scatter the leeks and carrots over the bottom of the plate and arrange the fish on this bed, then ring them with the cooked lettuce.

Cover and keep warm.

Cream the remaining 2 tablespoons of the butter with a fork and blend in a tablespoon of flour (only if the sauce is too thin). Dot the butter over the sauce off the heat, then bring to a boil, stirring for 1 minute. Add the cream, correct the seasoning, and pour over the fillets. Serve very hot. Extra sauce can be passed in a sauceboat.

NOTE: A good substitute is sea bream or bluefish. If you use bluefish fillets you need not remove the skins. In fact, leaving them on makes the fish easier to handle.

LAPIN AU CIDRE DE THIÉRACHE
Rabbit in cider

𝒮𝒮𝒮

SERVES 4 TO 6

1 rabbit, about 2½–3 pounds
flour
5 ounces (1¼ sticks) butter
1 tablespoon oil
4 shallots
1 bottle hard cider
thyme

bay leaf
salt and pepper
2 tablespoons currant jelly
6 medium firm-fleshed apples,
    peeled and cored
1 tablespoon extra-fine sugar

Cut the rabbit into serving pieces. The anatomy is unfamiliar and you will find that the most natural divisions are two pieces for each hind leg, two for the breast, and four for the saddle and the forelegs—one piece on each side with the ribs and one with each front leg. Dust with flour and shake well to knock off any excess.

In a heavy-bottomed casserole melt 2 tablespoons of the butter, add the oil, then add the pieces of rabbit. Cook over moderate heat until they are golden, taking care not to burn the fat.

Add the shallots, whole, and let them cook, stirring constantly, then pour in the cider to come to the top of the meat. Add thyme, a bay leaf, and salt and pepper. Cover and simmer over low heat for 30–40 minutes or more, depending on the size of the rabbit.

When the meat is done remove it from the casserole and keep it warm in a serving dish. The cooking juices should have been thickened by the flour in which you dredged the rabbit, but if they still seem too thin mix a teaspoon more of flour very thoroughly with the currant jelly and off the heat stir it into the juices with a wire whisk. Add the jelly alone if the sauce is thick enough. Bring to a boil for 2–3 minutes, stirring constantly. Replace the rabbit in the sauce to reheat.

Meanwhile, sauté the apples in the remaining 4 ounces (1 stick) butter, sprinkling them with the sugar to give them a beautiful golden glaze. Serve with the rabbit and sauce.

OMELETTE SURPRISE FLAMBÉE
Flaming surprise omelette

$\mathscr{S}\mathscr{S}\mathscr{S}$

SERVES 6

8-inch sponge or pound cake	1 quart vanilla ice cream
tangerine liqueur	6 eggs
⅔ cup blanched almonds	6 tablespoons extra-fine sugar

To prepare and serve this dessert choose a long dish which will go from the oven to the freezer. One hour before you plan to serve cut the cake into a rectangle 8 inches long by 2½ inches wide. Save the scraps.

Center the rectangle on the dish and moisten with the liqueur.

Chop the nuts roughly, then put them into a dry frying pan and cook until they turn golden, but be careful not to let them brown. Cool them and sprinkle half of them on the cake.

Cut the ice cream to fit the cake and crust it with the remaining nuts. Then mask completely with the cake scraps so that no ice cream shows. Place in the freezer set at the coldest setting.

Turn the oven on to its highest setting and let it heat for 30 minutes. Meanwhile separate the eggs. Beat the whites and as soon as they begin to be white add the sugar a little at a time. Continue beating and adding sugar until the whites are very stiff. The success of this dessert depends on the stiffness of the whites.

Stir the yolks just to mix and fold them carefully into the whites.

Just before you are ready to put the dessert into the oven spread three-quarters of the eggs over the ice cream with a spatula. Use the reserved quarter of the eggs to decorate with a pastry tube, making sure as you do that all the ice cream is well covered with meringue.

Arrange some sort of heatproof block in the oven—a turned-over cake pan with a piece of asbestos or tile on top works well—then put the dessert on top of that so the bottom doesn't get too hot. Watch carefully—the meringue should color in a few minutes. To serve, sprinkle with warmed tangerine liqueur and set alight, basting with the flames as you would a plum pudding.

N o t e : You can use any fruit liqueur you prefer for this dish.

TARTE À LA DUFLOT
Apple tart

✐✐✐

This tart is named for M. Duflot, counsel general of the region and nurseryman, who harvests the famous Boskup apples with the wonderful native tang of the soil.

Pâte brisée
1½ cups flour
6 ounces (1½ sticks) butter,
   softened
1 large pinch salt
1 pinch sugar
1 egg

4 apples

Filling
1 cup crème fraîche
1 tablespoon flour
1 tablespoon applejack or any
   apple-flavored eau-de-vie
1 egg

Preheat oven to 450°F.

Butter a 10-inch cake tin or flan dish.

Rapidly knead the flour with the softened butter, salt, sugar, and 1 tablespoon water. When these are all roughly amalgamated, knead in 1 egg. Roll out the dough twice to make sure it is well integrated, then place in the buttered pan.

Peel and core the apples and cut each into 8 sections. Arrange on the crust in concentric circles.

Mix the ingredients for the filling and pour over the middle of the apples, then spread to even out. Bake for 25–30 minutes, until the custard is set and golden and the crust browned.

Serve warm accompanied by a pot of thick crème fraîche and some extra-fine sugar.

NOTE : Although the pan is lined with crust, you cannot use a flan ring for this recipe, as the custard will work through and leak out. A cake pan is fine, but makes it hard to present, so the most elegant container is probably a flan dish with a removable bottom; you can serve it on just the bottom with the sides removed.

LUCIENNE DREBET

❀❀❀

Chez Georges
Lyon 1ᵉʳ

A real, an authentic charcuterie such as hardly exists in Lyon. Ten decorated tables and the cashier's desk where the proprietess is enthroned.

She is Lucienne, beautiful, elegant, and well coiffed. The door to the kitchen is open and she is marching between her cupboards and her stove—a modest cooking instrument run on gas. Here there is no printed menu, not even a hand-written one. When Lucienne has completed the inventory of her cupboards, she herself, pencil in hand, recites to you the contents of her larder. Grieved, she has no more boudin. Her pure, fresh Lyonnaise veal sausages cannot be confused with anyone else's. They are seasoned with mustard and soaked in Viré white wine. Tripe, certainly, but also calves' liver, which she knows the origin of and of which she says: "cooked in a frying pan in butter, finished in a shallot reduction with a thin stream of vinegar."

What would Lyonnaise cuisine be without vinegar? Judiciously employed, of course.

The star is Lucienne alone, skillet in hand, attacking a block of butter, poking here, shaking her vinegar bottle— leader of an invisible orchestra.

Her assistant is her son, stumbling on his dog, a cynic who disapproves of him. Not for anything in the world would he leave his place right at the narrow service door. While one waits here comes a bottle of red Viré, a cool, ripe Mâcon, and salad bowls. Here the term hors d'oeuvre is pronounced *salad bowls*. Smoked and salted herrings swimming in their marinade, potatoes in oil, sheep's trotters with seasoned mayonnaise, sliced cervelat sausages vinaigrette, garnished with rosettes, sausages of Lyon, of the world, Dauphine ham—I forget what else.

Lucienne thinks that everyone could make what she has made. The recipes? But they aren't special. Yes, Lucienne, they are precious, your everyday recipes—simple, savory, coddled, reassuring woman's cooking prepared with the most authentic simplicity—that of quality.

LA CERVELLE DE CANUT
Canut "brains"

𝒮𝒮𝒮

MAKES ABOUT 2 CUPS

1½ cups *fromage blanc*, drained (see note)

salt and pepper

minced fresh herbs of the season, such as chives, chervil, parsley, tarragon, dill, etc.

garlic

dry white wine

⅓ cup heavy cream

vinegar

oil

Beat the *fromage blanc* to soften it. This is an important step, so don't neglect it. Salt and pepper the cheese, then add the herbs with a splinter of garlic, no more. Add the herbs spoonful by spoonful so you can stop as soon as the cheese has completely enveloped them and they can hardly be seen anymore. The cheese is edible as is, but the connoisseurs improve it by adding—carefully so as not to soften it too much—1 or 2 spoonfuls of white wine (a Viré or Mâconnais for instance), several spoonfuls of cream, and a thin stream of vinegar, then a teaspoon or two of oil.

Stir to mix these into the cheese and to give it a good consistency; it should be melting but not liquid. If necessary add more salt, pepper, and herbs to reinforce the seasoning.

This is at its best served with thin slices of good toast.

NOTE: *Fromage blanc* can be bought in France easily. Here, you have to make your own, but it's simple. In a blender combine 15 ounces (1½ cups—one container) *whole*-milk ricotta with 4 tablespoons plain yogurt and a pinch of salt. Blend until very smooth, then refrigerate for 12 hours. Before using it in this recipe wrap it in cheesecloth in a sieve and allow to drain (it may not need to) for 2–3 hours.

RIS DE VEAU AUX MORILLES
Sweetbreads with morels

SERVES 4

4 fresh sweetbreads
6 ounces (1½ sticks) butter
salt and pepper
3 ounces dried morels, or better,
1 pound fresh morels
½ cup heavy cream

Contrary to the usual procedure, don't soak the sweetbreads. Instead, using patience and a small knife, relieve them of their skins and wastes, but keep their shape. Then, over low heat, cook them in a frying pan with plenty of butter (about 4 ounces). Both the butter and the sweetbreads should remain golden and not brown. Salt and pepper to taste.

If you are using dried morels swish them around vigorously in tepid water so any hidden grains of sand in their creases will rinse out. Then let them soak in tepid water to inflate for 2 hours. If you are using fresh morels you don't have to soak them, but do wash them even more carefully.

Once the dried mushrooms are inflated treat dried and fresh the same.

Sauté them in the remaining 2 ounces of butter, then cover with the cream. Add salt and pepper. Let simmer until the cream coats each mushroom.

Put the sweetbreads and the morels together and cook gently for 10–15 minutes so they can exchange their juices. Then serve.

POITRINE DE VEAU BRAISÉE
Braised breast of veal

ℐℐℐ

SERVES 6 TO 8

4 ounces (1 stick) butter
4½-pound breast of veal (with
   bones)
3 onions, roughly chopped
1 bouquet garni (parsley,
   thyme, rosemary, bay leaf)

In an iron cocotte melt half the butter and over low heat brown the breast of veal all in one piece. In principle the butter shouldn't burn, but if it does, when the meat is browned, discard the burned butter before continuing with the recipe, and melt the remaining 2 ounces.

Add the onions, bouquet garni, and a tablespoon of water. Cover the cocotte and cook over very low heat for 2 hours, turning the meat once. The bones in a breast of veal are really cartilage and will come apart easily. Serve cut apart with the cooking juices and accompanied by macaroni and cheese (see following recipe).

GRATIN DE MACARONI DE LUCIENNE
Lucienne's macaroni and cheese

𝒟𝒟𝒟

SERVES 6

10 ounces (about 4 cups) large
  macaroni—big shells, lasagna
  noodles, etc.
4 cups milk
1 cup cream

⅓ cup grated Gruyère or
  Swiss cheese
2 ounces (½ stick) butter
salt and pepper

The day before you are going to serve this dish cook the macaroni in a large pot of boiling salted water to which a tablespoon of oil has been added. Cook until it is *al dente*, that is, firm without being crunchy. When it is done, turn it out into a colander and refresh under cold running water. It should become almost cold.

While macaroni is cooking, scald and cool the milk. When milk is cool put the macaroni into a gratin dish, pour the milk over it, and refrigerate overnight.

To cook, heat the gratin dish on top of the stove. Let the milk come to a boil again over medium heat and cook until it evaporates a bit. While the dish is on top of the stove preheat your oven to 300°F. When some of the milk has evaporated and been absorbed, pour in about half the cream, then sprinkle on the grated cheese and dot with the butter. Salt and pepper to taste.

Put the dish into the oven and bake for about 20 minutes. Keep an eye on it and if the tops of the pasta seem to be drying out add more cream. The liquid should bubble up again, and it is ready when the butter, cheese, milk, and cream have all been absorbed or amalgamated into a thick sauce.

JEANNE DROUIN

Auberge du Grand Saint-Pierre
Les Haies à Charmes, Dourlers (Nord)

A handsome Flemish woman, solid as a rock, setting her brow into all tempests—too brief a description of a unique woman.

She describes her adventure, which began in Avesnes in

1955 in an old inn at the sign of Saint Pierre. It was absolutely lacking in any of the amenities:

"Culinarily we were unencumbered by knowledge. My husband was a publicist. I had left the Valenciennes Beaux-Arts, but I had already tried my wings in an elegant grocery store where I prepared the take-out platters.

"I'll never forget our folkloric beginning. One day around Easter—we had hardly settled in, the stove was rickety and wheezy—all of a sudden the house was full. An indescribable mess. Do you think that 'They' left? No, these Belgians took matters in hand. One blew on the fire, one made change; it was like a Flemish village fair. We thought the night was hopeless. One would not care to relive that opening.

"That's all far behind us now. Michelin has discovered us."

The gifted, inexperienced chef made progress, and passed all the stages to reach two stars. This is cooking outside the realm of professionalism.

"One can't expend one's energy limitlessly, ceaselessly, without endangering one's health. I had to slow myself down.

"We built our new establishment so that we could finally have the space we'd been missing. Times changed, problems arose pitilessly. We faced them. Our stars paled one moment, then returned with a bang. The children grew up. With the help of my daughter, Claudine, and my young Bernard, I've gotten back all my energy and enthusiasm.

"To catch our breath we inaugurated at the end of 1972 a cycle of various shows and events scheduled from November to April. In the cultural desert of our region the public, which is often expert, has acquired a taste for it. We made every effort to get the cooperation of well-known artists and we also had recourse to the often surprising and neglected regional resources."

Jeanne takes on all this in addition to her cooking—divided between typical local preparations and specialties created long ago.

She doesn't have to be rejuvenated to be in the contemporary mode. Jeanne Drouin mastered cooking long ago, keeping the tastes of things as they are in accord with Curnonsky's fine formula for woman's cooking.

She confided some of these secrets to me.

FLAMICHE AU MAROILLES
Cheese tart

ꞵ ꞵ ꞵ

FOR A 9- OR 10-INCH PIE PLATE
SERVES 6 AS A FIRST COURSE, 2 HUNGRY OR
4 DAINTY EATERS AS A MAIN COURSE

2 packages yeast

2 tablespoons scalded milk,
   cooled to room temperature

1⅔ cups flour

1 pinch salt

1 pinch sugar

1 egg

1 tablespoon peanut oil

3 ounces (¾ stick) butter

1 ripe Maroilles cheese

pepper

Butter the pie plate and set aside.

Dissolve the yeast in the milk.

Pour the flour onto the table, make a well, and into the well place the yeast and all the other ingredients except the cheese and pepper.

Mix with your hands. Knead, push, beat, and pull the dough on the table until it is smooth and supple without being soft and pulls away from your hands and the table when kneaded. Form into a ball. It should hold its shape and not flatten out.

Keeping it round, roll the dough to the dimensions of the pie plate, then place it on the plate. Remove the crust from the cheese and place it in the middle of the dough. Leave a ½-inch margin of dough around the cheese on the bottom of the plate (not counting the sides). If the cheese doesn't fill this area, slice it in half crosswise and cut one half into strips to fill in around the edges. Pepper generously.

Cover with a towel or a piece of plastic and set aside in a warm place for 1 hour. The dough should double in volume.

Place in a very hot oven (450°F.) for 8–10 minutes. The well-cooked dough should have a crusty surface and the cheese should be melted.

Serve hot with butter on the table, and let any person who wants to butter his piece to his own taste.

NOTE : Maroilles cheese is difficult to find. It is imported into this country only in November and December and then not everywhere. A very good substitute is a ripe Pont l'Évêque.

COQ À LA BIÈRE
Chicken in beer

✑✑✑

SERVES 6 TO 8

9 ounces bacon (about 12 slices)
1 large roasting chicken or two
   5-pound fowls
flour
1 tablespoon bacon fat or oil
3 medium onions, halved
3 shallots

2 cups beer
1 pinch thyme
1 bay leaf
salt and pepper
1 tablespoon cornstarch
   (optional)
2 ounces (½ stick) butter

Cut the bacon into matchstick-size bits if it is one piece or into 1-inch pieces if it is sliced. Blanch for 5 minutes in boiling water.

Cut the chicken into serving pieces, then dredge lightly in flour, shaking off the excess. Heat the bacon fat or oil in a large iron casserole over moderate heat, then brown the chicken parts lightly with the onions, shallots, and blanched bacon.

Add the beer, thyme, bay leaf, and salt and pepper and cover the casserole. Simmer over low heat until the chicken is tender; this should be about 1½ hours for the large roasting chicken and 2–3 hours for the fowls.

Chicken in beer isn't a stew and the sauce will remain thin. If it seems to be thickening too much add a little boiling water.

The small amount of flour used during the preparation of the chicken should be enough to give the sauce some body so that it is more a sauce than a stock, but if you prefer it thicker you can blend 1 tablespoon of cornstarch into ½ tablespoon of butter and add it with the rest of the butter.

To serve, remove the chicken pieces and arrange them in a serving bowl with the onions and shallots (discard the bay leaf). Bring the sauce to a boil, then turn off the heat and little by little stir in the butter (either with the cornstarch or not). This is what gives the sauce its smoothness and sparkle. Pour over the chicken and serve hot.

BALLOTTINE DE LAPIN AU BANYULS
Stuffed rabbit

𝒮 𝒮 𝒮

SERVES 6 TO 8

1 rabbit, about 3 pounds
1 pork caul (from a pork
    butcher)

Stuffing

1½ ounces (3 tablespoons)
  butter
1 shallot, minced
the rabbit's liver, minced
¾ cup bread crumbs
½ cup milk
4 ounces chopped veal
4 ounces fine sausage meat
1 egg

1 ounce (¼ cup) seedless
  raisins
1 tablespoon brandy
1 tablespoon dry Banyuls
  (Bordeaux)
salt and pepper
nutmeg
coriander

For this dish you need a rabbit that is skinned and boned and still in one piece. Try to get your butcher to do it for you.

Melt the butter in a large skillet and cook the shallots but don't let them brown. Then add the minced liver and let it stiffen.

Meanwhile, soak the bread crumbs in the milk until they have absorbed it, and when they have, mix them and all the other stuffing ingredients together and season very highly.

Spread the rabbit out on a table and place the stuffing all along the back. Fold the flesh over and around so that it looks like a big sausage. Wash the caul fat in warm, salted water and dry it. Wrap the rabbit-sausage in the caul fat and tie it up as though it were a rolled roast—loosely the long way, firmly the round way. Cut off any extra caul fat, as it will put too much fat into the sauce.

Cooking

2 tablespoons goose fat or lard	1 tablespoon brandy
15 shallots, minced	1 cup Bordeaux
7 ounces mushrooms, quartered	2 tablespoons heavy cream
1 sprig thyme	1 teaspoon cornstarch dissolved
1 bay leaf	in a little cold water
salt and pepper	juice of ½ lemon

In a large, heavy casserole heat the fat or lard and slowly brown the rabbit on all sides, being careful not to let the fat burn. Add the shallots, mushrooms, thyme, bay leaf, brandy, and Bordeaux. Salt and pepper to taste.

Cover and let simmer for 1½–2 hours.

To serve, cut the string, slice the rabbit-sausage and arrange it on a heated serving platter and keep warm.

Strain the cooking sauce and skim off any excess fat. Return to the casserole with the cream, the cornstarch dissolved in water, and the lemon juice. Heat, and serve a little poured over the rabbit and the rest separately in a sauceboat. Accompany with potatoes, either boiled or sliced and fried in goose fat.

Cold, this dish is just as good.

N o t e : If you can't get caul fat substitute a piece of cheesecloth, dampened, then wrung out and wrapped around the rabbit. Tie it as you would the caul-wrapped rabbit, then paint the outside lavishly with rendered goose fat or bacon fat (goose is preferable). Before serving remove the cloth.

ESCALOPES MAÎTRE PIERRE
Veal scallops with tomato sauce

♫ ♫ ♫

SERVES 6

6 veal scallops

Coating

2 eggs
1 scant tablespoon olive oil
¾ cup flour
salt and pepper
1 cup bread crumbs

Tomato sauce

1 pound onions, finely chopped	marjoram
2 tablespoons olive oil	oregano
1¾ pounds tomatoes, peeled, seeded, and chopped	savory
1 chicken liver, finely chopped	fennel
2–3 sprigs rosemary	2 tablespoons port
	salt and pepper

Cooking

½ cup olive oil
1 cup crème fraîche
3 tablespoons grated Gruyère or
  Swiss cheese

Begin by making the tomato sauce, which has to simmer for
2 hours.

Put the chopped onions and the 2 tablespoons olive oil into a heavy-bottomed pot and cook slowly so the onions don't burn. When they are soft, add the tomatoes, the pieces of chicken liver, rosemary (which must be used with discretion), and a pinch of all the other herbs (or a sprig if fresh) and the port. Cook very slowly, covered, until the mixture becomes a thick paste. There should be about 6 good tablespoons. Add salt and pepper. This can be done well ahead of time and kept in the refrigerator and reheated.

Just before you are ready to serve, heat the ½ cup olive oil in a large skillet.

Make the coating by beating the 2 eggs with the scant tablespoon of oil in a wide shallow bowl. Then pour some flour, mixed with salt and pepper, onto a piece of waxed paper and put on one side of the egg bowl. Pour the bread crumbs onto another piece of waxed paper and place on the other side. Prepare the veal scallops by dredging them first in the seasoned flour, then dipping them in the eggs, and finally dredging them in the bread crumbs. As each scallop is coated, drop it into the hot oil. Turn once. These don't take very long to cook, and the first should be golden and cooked by the time the last goes into the pan. As each scallop is ready, remove it from the oil, drain it, and arrange it on an ovenproof platter.

"Butter" each scallop with the tomato sauce, then spoon the crème fraîche over them, and finally sprinkle with the grated cheese. Brown the tops rapidly under the broiler.

Serve with fresh buttered noodles.

NOTE: To make your own bread crumbs crumble or grate some stale bread, then dry out the crumbs in the oven without letting them brown.

GÂTEAU AUX NOIX AU RHUM
Rum-flavored nut tart

This recipe won the Grande Poêle d'Or award for Jeanne Drouin in 1966.

> 1 tablespoon butter
> 4 ounces pâte feuilletée, turned
>   four times (see note)
> apricot jam

Butter the pan or tart mold with the tablespoon of butter, then line it with the pâte feuilletée. Heat the apricot jam in a small saucepan and stir to get it to a spreadable consistency. Glaze the inside of the pastry with a thin layer of jam. When the pastry is glazed set the shell aside in the refrigerator.

Nut cream

9 ounces (2⅓ cups) finely
  chopped walnuts
1¼ cups extra-fine sugar
4 ounces (1 stick) butter,
  softened

1 tablespoon crème fraîche
1½ tablespoons vanilla sugar
2 generous tablespoons rum
4 eggs, separated

Preheat the oven to 400°F.

Mix together all the ingredients except the egg whites. Beat the whites into stiff peaks, then carefully fold them into the rest of the ingredients.

Fill the chilled pastry shell with the nut mixture and smooth the top.

Place on the lowest rack of the oven and bake until the bottom is crusty and crisp and the top is lightly browned. This will take about 50 minutes. Don't open the oven door to check until then or the filling, raised by the egg whites, might collapse.

Cool on a rack while you make the glaze.

Glaze

rum
4 tablespoons confectioners'
    sugar
apricot jam, heated and
    strained
12 green walnuts (see note)

Stir enough rum into the sugar to make it runny but not liquid. With a pastry brush lightly coat the top of the tart with the heated and strained apricot jam. Mix the rum and confectioners' sugar and pour over the apricot layer. Smooth with a spatula or small table knife.

Decorate with green walnuts at regular intervals.

Notes: You might want to try Huguette Meliet's recipe for pâte feuilletée on pp. 234–36.

If you cannot find green walnuts, regular brown ones are a perfectly acceptable substitute.

FERNANDE EUZET

Le Pistou
Paris 13ᵉ

Fernande Euzet is the type of intrepid woman who says that circumstances pushed her, forgetting that she gave them the final shove.

She is from the Southwest, whose rich, savory products have awakened so many talents, from thatched cottage to château. Why Le Pistou? Because having meridional roots, too, she appreciated that flavorsome Niçoise soup. It is featured on her menu during fresh basil season (Easter to frost).

The herb also goes into the Sorges sauce, named for a little village between Thiviers and Périgueux in the Dordogne. She got the recipe from the repertoire of her friend Madame Leymaire, another famous woman chef.

Her restaurant is the kind of Paris bistro where one has to book a table to come and taste cooking strongly marked with a simple, flavorful provincialism—real woman's cooking.

From the time she first opened her restaurant she was already a "mère" with her plats du jour, repeated so often that one won't dine at Le Pistou without sampling Fernande Euzet's canard Françoise after the moules à l'Arlésienne. Her terrines, her desserts on display during the main course, create nothing less than euphoria.

SUÇARELLES

ℐℐℐ

These are gray snails in their shells. Because they are served in a delicious sauce, one sucks at them. Hence the name (probably). The French for "suck" is *sucer*.

They are available in 2-pound tins, preserved in their cooking juices in their shells. Fernande Euzet says that those from the Alps are the best.

6 tablespoons olive oil

10 ounces (about 1½ medium) onions, minced

7 ounces anchovy fillets, packed in oil

½ cup grated Gruyère or Swiss cheese

⅔ cup (5 ounces) almonds with their skins, coarsely ground

¾ pound tomatoes, peeled, seeded, and chopped

pepper

1 small pinch cayenne

1 pinch thyme

1 sprig rosemary

1 bay leaf

5 ounces fatback, minced in a blender or food processor

Heat the olive oil in a large saucepan and cook the onions over low heat until they are soft, but don't let them brown. When they are soft, add the drained anchovies and cook, stirring constantly, for 3–4 minutes, then sprinkle in the cheese. The result should have a soft, pâté-like consistency.

Add the almonds, then the tomatoes. (In winter, when tomatoes are tasteless, reinforce the flavor with a good tablespoon of tomato paste.)

Add pepper, cayenne, thyme, rosemary, and bay leaf. Bring the sauce to a rolling boil, add 1 cup boiling water, then continue to boil over high heat so the elements don't separate. While it boils add the minced fatback and cook for 10–12 minutes, until the fat dissolves a bit. Add the well-drained snails, and when the sauce returns to a boil and the snails bob up, take the pot off the heat and set it aside to rest and absorb for about 20 minutes.

Hot or cold, these snails are delicious (if messy) hors d'oeuvres.

TERRINE DE VEAU ET DE PORC
Veal and pork pâté

✑ ✑ ✑

1½ pounds pork fillet
1½ pounds veal round
2 carrots, sliced
2 medium onions, sliced
salt and pepper
nutmeg
parsley
thyme sprigs
1 large bay leaf
1 bottle dry white wine

½ cup dry Madeira
4 tablespoons olive oil
1 piece caul fat or enough
    blanched bacon to line the
    bottom and sides of the
    terrine
1 pound pork shoulder, finely
    chopped
1 pound veal (any cut), finely
    chopped

Cut the pork fillet and the veal round into very thin slices. This is easier to do if you place the meat in the freezer long enough to harden it, but not until it is solid. Put the slices in a large glass or crockery bowl with the sliced carrots and onions, salt and pepper, and a large pinch of nutmeg. Strew in some unchopped parsley, thyme, and the bay leaf. Pour in enough wine to cover the meat, then add the Madeira and olive oil. Stir to mix, then place in the refrigerator for 8–10 hours to marinate. Stir to turn things over two or three times.

Preheat oven to 400°F.

Arrange the caul fat or blanched bacon to line the bottom and sides of the terrine. Strain the marinade and reserve. Mix together the chopped meats with a little salt, pepper, and nutmeg. Arrange a third of it on the bottom of the terrine, then moisten with 2 tablespoons of the strained marinade; cover with half the meat slices (use both kinds), then 2 more tablespoons of marinade. Repeat layering of chopped meat and meat slices, moistening between layers. Top with the rest of the chopped meat. When you have finished, add enough marinade so that it shows around the sides at the top of the terrine, then cover the terrine with a piece of aluminum foil. Place the covered terrine in a large, shallow ovenproof dish and pour in hot (not boiling) water so that it comes halfway up the sides of the terrine. Place in the preheated oven.

If it looks as though the water in the bain marie is going to boil, lower the heat. It should never do more than quiver, or the texture of the pâté will be spoiled. Help the marinade penetrate by pricking the meats, and if necessary add more as the pâté cooks. Cook for 2½ hours.

Remove from the oven and place the terrine on a rack to cool. When it is warm, but not hot, press down gently on the meat with your palms. Cover the top with a flat piece of wood, then place weights on the wood that will prevent the cooling pâté from rising, but won't crush it—paperback books are good for this.

Let stand 24 hours before serving. If the weather is hot, place in the refrigerator to rest, but room temperature is preferable.

SAUCE DE SORGES
Sorges sauce

𝒮𝒮𝒮

1 lemon

1 teaspoon prepared Dijon or
  other fine mustard

salt and pepper

peanut oil (about ½ cup)

1 egg

1 tablespoon chopped shallots

2 tablespoons chervil (not
  chopped but cut with
  scissors)

½ tablespoon chopped tarragon

1 tablespoon finely chopped
  chives

Squeeze the lemon and set aside the juice.

Put the mustard in a small bowl, add a few drops of
lemon juice, and some salt and pepper. Beating with a wire
whisk as though you were making mayonnaise, add the oil
in a trickle over the mustard. The sauce should rise and
thicken as you whisk. From time to time add a few more
drops of lemon juice so the sauce remains emulsified.

Soft-boil an egg for exactly 3½ minutes, then add the
hot yolk to the sauce. Keep trickling in oil and whisking.
When you have about ¾ cup, add the herbs a little at a time,
one after the other. Correct the seasoning—the sauce should
be quite spicy.

Poach the white of the soft-boiled egg in simmering
water and when it is completely hard drain it, crush it with
the back of a fork, and add it to the sauce.

Gourmets make much of this sauce, which is an equally
good accompaniment for boiled vegetables such as artichokes, asparagus, or celeriac, or for boiled meats.

MOULES À L'ARLÉSIENNE
Mussels in tomato sauce

ℐℐℐ

12 ounces (3 sticks) butter
3 large leeks, whites only,
   chopped
3 carrots, grated
thyme
1 small bay leaf
salt and pepper

3 tomatoes, quartered
2 hard-boiled eggs
cayenne
nutmeg
8–9 cups mussels (about 2
   quarts or 4 pounds)

Take the butter out of the refrigerator. Melt 4 ounces of butter in a saucepan, then add the leeks, carrots, thyme, bay leaf, and salt and pepper. Cook over moderate heat until all the vegetables are softened, nearly cooked, then add the tomatoes.

Simmer until the mixture becomes a paste, then put through the fine blade of a vegetable mill with the hard-boiled eggs. Or if you don't have a vegetable mill you can liquefy it in a blender or food processor, then press through a sieve to remove any tomato skins or fiber.

Correct the seasoning and add a pinch of cayenne and nutmeg. This sauce should be spicy. Let it cool completely.

While the sauce is cooking, steam the mussels in a large pot with a little water until they open. Discard any that stay closed. Open the shells completely and discard the empty half of the shells. Arrange the shells on plates, mussel up, so they don't overlap.

Stir the remaining 8 ounces of butter (which has been

out of the refrigerator for about an hour by now) into the sauce, then spoon each shell full as you would with snail butter.

Set aside in the refrigerator until you are almost ready to serve, then quickly heat in the oven and serve immediately.

NOTE: A less elegant but much easier way to serve this dish is to spoon some of the sauce into each steamed-open mussel shell and let the guests dig with small forks.

CANARDS FRANÇOISE
Duck with onions, mushrooms, and raisins

𝒯 𝒯 𝒯

SERVES 6

2 ducks (the smallest you can find)

Stock (the basis of the sauce)

necks, wing tips, and giblets of
the ducks
chicken backs and necks
2 carrots
1 leek

1 bouquet garni (parsley,
thyme, ½ bay leaf)
2 stalks celery
⅔ cup raisins

Sauce

4 ounces (1 stick) butter
10 small white onions
12 shallots
1 tablespoon sugar
10 ounces (about 3 cups) small
mushrooms

1 lemon
2 tablespoons flour
7 ounces (10 slices) bacon, cut
into small pieces and blanched
salt and pepper

Stock

Put all the stock ingredients (except raisins) together in a stock pot with 6½ cups water. Cook for 1½ hours. Strain. Bring to a rapid boil and reduce to 1½ cups (about 15 minutes, so watch carefully). This will be the basis for your sauce. Add the raisins and set aside.

Preheat oven to 400°F.

Salt and pepper the cavities of the ducks and close the openings. Bend the tail down into the back cavity and pull the neck skin up over the front. Truss. Put the ducks into a roasting pan. Salt and pepper the outsides. Put into the oven and roast for about 1 hour and 15 minutes, piercing the skin occasionally so the fat can escape. Then turn the oven off, but leave the ducks in it with the door open while you prepare the sauce.

Sauce

Melt 5 tablespoons of the butter, then put the peeled but whole onions and shallots into it. Cook over high heat, stirring, and sprinkle with the sugar. Lower the heat, and, stirring often, let cook until the sugar has caramelized and the tip of a knife pierces the still-firm vegetables easily.

Trim the mushroom stems and wash them quickly in water to which you have added the juice of half a lemon. Cut the mushrooms into quarters, dry them, and cook them with the juice of half a lemon in the remaining 3 tablespoons of butter over moderate heat.

When the onions are ready, sprinkle them with a level tablespoon of flour and stir for 1 minute to mix. Then add the mushrooms and their juices, the reduced stock with the raisins, and the chopped bacon.

Bring to a boil, add salt and pepper, and keep hot, but don't cook any longer.

To serve cut each duck into quarters and keep warm on a heated serving platter. Get rid of as much fat as you can from the roasting pan, but try to keep all the juices and cooked-on bits. Deglaze the pan with 1 or 2 tablespoons boiling water or dry white wine, scraping up all the cooked-on bits with the back of a fork. Pour the juices into the sauce. Carefully reheat and spoon some over the ducks. Serve the rest separately in a sauceboat.

Because of the vegetables in the sauce you need not serve vegetables with this dish, but if you want to, any vegetable, from potatoes to peas, would be good.

MARTHE
FAURE

⚜⚜⚜

Auberge Saint-Quentinoise
Livry-Gargan
(Seine-Saint-Denis)

The Auberge Saint-Quentinoise, created by Marthe Faure's parents in 1907, is now over seventy years old. Wagons coming from the north to provision Paris stopped here, and people got up in the night to feed the horses—still more picturesquely, to heat the bricks and foot warmers for the passengers. Time passed and stagecoaches were replaced with buses. In 1918 Marthe's mother held onto the restaurant.

The wholesale butchers in nearby La Villette came to feast themselves on her rabbit fricassee, stewed slowly since dawn, on her stews, and so many other flavorsome preparations. They hardly recognized the new, bright, rich, comfortable inn that Marthe and her husband installed within the walls of the old one in 1968.

Marthe tells of how the work was barely finished when she lost her husband and had to take charge alone. She quickly discovered that she was up to it.

Like her mother, she reigns as chef in the kitchen. With better help, no doubt, the inn has changed, the food evolved.

The cooking is both sophisticated and simple. With all the top-quality produce from fine sources there is no need to disguise it to make it distinguished. From her fresh salmon steak on a bed of sorrel, suprêmes of sole with cucumbers, through her sweetbreads, her veal kidneys, her meats, to the beautiful palette of desserts where parfaits frozen from fruits of the season dominate—each is her work, each a success.

She has received awards such as the palms of the Cordon Bleu de France, being named Chevalière du Mérite Agricole, and winning the first Grand Prize of the Poêle d'Or. All of these titles, conferred by an impartial jury, attest to her talents.

Her cellar is rich in venerable bottles, but doesn't neglect the young wines of good years and good soils. Her excellent champagnes add a solid attraction to her menu, which begins with this elegant phrase:

"This week we recommend. . . ."

SUPRÊMES DE SOLES AUX CONCOMBRES
Fillets of sole with cucumbers

ꝸ ꝸ ꝸ

SERVES 6

6 sole, about 1 pound each	1 cup dry white wine
1 carrot	¾ cup heavy cream
1 leek	salt and pepper
2 stalks celery	3 egg yolks
1 onion	2 cucumbers
1 bouquet garni (parsley, thyme, bay leaf)	2 ounces (½ stick) butter
	1 tablespoon minced parsley

Ask your fish man to fillet the sole for you and to return the trimmings (the backs and heads and tails) to you to make the stock.

Make your stock from these trimmings, the vegetables, the bouquet garni, 6 cups of water, and the wine (Muscadet or Chablis is a good choice). Cook for 25 minutes, then strain.

Pour the strained stock into a large shallow pan such as a *sautoir*, add half the cream, and heat. Gently press the fillets on the side where the skin was with a spatula to flatten them, then poach them in two or three batches—so they don't overlap. The liquid should just be on the verge of simmering, and the fish should cook only 1 or 2 minutes, just to firm.

Set the fillets aside on a buttered platter. Spoon a little of the cooking liquid over them, and cover them so they stay warm but don't continue to cook.

Strain the liquid again, then reduce it to 1 cup and correct seasoning.

Prepare the cucumber balls as below.

Beat the yolks with the rest of the cream in a small saucepan, then slowly add the reduced stock, stirring constantly. Over low heat continue to stir and let the sauce thicken as you would a custard until it coats a wooden spoon. Don't let it boil, but be fearless about letting it thicken—three yolks in 1 cup of liquid should make a nice, velvety sauce. Drain the fillets and spoon the sauce over them. Decorate the platter with the cucumber balls and serve the rest of the sauce in a sauceboat.

Cucumber balls

Peel the cucumbers, then use a melon baller to make them into little balls. Poach in boiling salted water until they can be pierced with the point of a knife. Drain the cucumbers, place in a frying pan with the butter, cook gently without letting them take on color for 12–15 minutes, then sprinkle with the parsley.

To serve, remove from the butter with a slotted spoon and arrange in little heaps on the platter with the fillets of sole.

PINTADEAUX DES ÎLES
Guinea fowl as prepared in the islands

✑ ✑ ✑

SERVES 6

½ cup rum
1 cup Smyrna raisins
2 guinea fowl, about 2 pounds
   each
2 bananas
salt and pepper

6 ounces (1½ sticks) butter
1 tablespoon peanut oil
pineapple
1 tablespoon confectioners'
   sugar

Warm the rum and plump the raisins in it for about 2 hours.

Using your fingers pull the skin away from, but not off, the breasts of the birds, being careful not to tear it. Drain a quarter of the raisins and stuff them into the cavities you have created on either side of the breastbone.

Dice the bananas into small pieces, add salt and pepper, and put half into the cavity of each bird. Also stuff about a tablespoon of butter into each cavity and a few more raisins.

Sew the birds closed again. Close both ends and tie their wings and legs down against their bodies.

In a heavy casserole large enough to hold both birds without crowding, melt 4 ounces of butter and add the peanut oil. When the fat is hot, add the birds.

Over low heat, brown the birds on all sides, turning two or three times. Add salt and pepper and a tablespoon of hot water, and cover the pot. Lower the heat so that the birds can cook very slowly for 40–50 minutes.

Just before the cooking time is up, drain the rest of the

raisins and set them aside, and reheat the rum. Remove the guinea fowl to a heatproof dish, sprinkle the heated rum over them, and flame.

Carve each fowl into four pieces: two legs and two breasts with wings. Arrange on a heated serving plate and divide the banana stuffing around them. Pour any rum and juices from the carving plate into the cooking juices, then spoon this very hot sauce over the birds or serve separately in a sauceboat.

To garnish the platter, peel and core a pineapple, then slice into rings. Or use half a tin of canned pineapple rings in syrup, well drained. Brown the rings in the remaining butter in a large frying pan and sprinkle with confectioners' sugar. Add the reserved raisins and let them heat with the pineapple.

The butter and sugar will caramelize the pineapple rings and make them golden. Arrange them around the birds on the serving platter.

NOTES: This dish can also be made with chicken. Use two small roasting chickens and follow the same instructions.

The banana stuffing almost disappears in the cooking, although it tastes delicious. You may want to make a little more in the oven. If so, purée 4 bananas with 1 stick of butter and add quite a bit of salt and pepper. Bake at 350°F. for about 40 minutes or until browned and crusty on top.

ROGNONS DE VEAU DU PRINCE
Veal kidneys for a prince

SSS

These veal kidneys are flamed with bourbon, arranged on crêpes folded into turnovers, and covered with their creamy sauce.

This sauce won the Grand Prix of the Poêle d'Or in 1968 for its inventor, Marthe Faure.

4 ounces golden Smyrna raisins	Worcestershire sauce
¼ cup bourbon	1 ladleful veal stock
2 large, handsome veal kidneys,	⅔ cup crème fraîche
or 3 medium ones	1 pinch dry mustard
4 ounces (1 stick) butter	1 pinch powdered sage

Crèpes

3 eggs
1 cup flour
1 pinch salt
1 tablespoon vegetable oil
1 cup milk

Soak the raisins in the bourbon. Prepare the crêpe batter at least 2 hours before you plan to make the crêpes. The crêpes can be made a day before you plan to use them.

To make the batter mix the eggs together and drop them into a well in the middle of the flour with a pinch of salt and the oil. Little by little add the milk to get a fluid batter. If the batter has thickened while standing, add a little more milk, and just before you cook the crêpes add half the steeped raisins, but no liquid.

Make the crêpes very light and thin and about 7 inches in diameter. If you made them larger than that you can cut them back to size. If you are keeping them for any length of time, don't let them dry out. As soon as they are cool, wrap them in aluminum foil with pieces of waxed paper between them.

Ask your butcher to pare the kidneys, that is to cut the fat and cord away. But don't have him slice them ahead of time—that should be done at the last minute.

When you are ready to cook the kidneys, cut them into slices about ½ inch thick. In a large frying pan heat a little butter, but don't let it sizzle, and sauté the kidneys rapidly. Flame them with half the bourbon until they no longer look half raw. Add several drops of Worcestershire sauce. Set the kidneys aside, with their juices, on a hot plate covered with a piece of buttered waxed paper.

Deglaze the cooking pot with a small ladle of veal stock. Bring it to a boil, then add the crème fraîche and dry mustard. Add the sage.

Reduce until the cream coats a wooden spoon.

Heat a little fresh butter in a skillet and use it to reheat the slices of kidney quickly. Add the rest of the steeped raisins and the rest of the bourbon and flame a last time. Pour the juice into the waiting sauce, and bring to a boil.

Arrange the crêpes on a serving platter and put a sixth of the kidneys on each. Spoon the boiling sauce over them one at a time and fold each crêpe up in the hot sauce. When all the crêpes are filled and folded, spoon the rest of the sauce over them. Cover the dish with aluminum foil and place in a very hot oven for a moment to reheat. Serve very hot.

GIBELOTTE MÈRE DE FRANCE
Mère de France's rabbit fricassee

Ữ Ữ Ữ

SERVES 6

1 rabbit, about 3 pounds

Marinade

1 carrot, sliced
1 onion, quartered
1 bouquet garni (thyme,
   parsley, bay leaf, a sprig of
   savory)

1½ bottles dry white wine
   (such as Muscadet)
salt
10 peppercorns

Cut the rabbit into pieces. Rabbit anatomy is unfamiliar and the most natural way to cut it is into two pieces for each hind leg, two for the breast, and four for the saddle and two front legs—one piece on each side with the ribs, and one with the front leg. Marinate for several hours with the carrot, onion, bouquet garni, wine to cover, and salt and peppercorns.

Cooking

5 ounces salt pork, cut into
   small pieces
4 ounces (1 stick) butter
2 shallots
1 clove garlic

5 ounces lean bacon
12 small onions
1 tablespoon flour
1 teaspoon butter

In a large frying pan render the salt pork. Remove the rabbit from the marinade (save the marinade, though), dry the meat, and brown it on all sides over moderate heat. Remove from the pan and drain.

Heat the butter in a casserole and add the rabbit. Strain the marinade into a saucepan and heat it, then add it to the rabbit in the casserole. Save the bouquet garni from the strained marinade. If necessary, add more white wine to the casserole until the meat is covered, then add the shallots, and crush the clove of garlic into the casserole. Finally add the bouquet garni reserved from the marinade. Cover and simmer until the pieces of rabbit are cooked, probably about 1½ hours, but check after an hour. You should be able to pierce them easily with a fork.

Remove the meat from the cooking liquid and keep warm. Cut the bacon into small pieces and blanch it with the little onions in boiling water for 5 minutes. Add both to the stock and reduce it to about half. Work the flour into the teaspoon of butter until it forms a paste, then add it, bit by bit, to the sauce, off the heat. Return to medium-high heat and, stirring constantly, cook until the sauce thickens.

Return the rabbit to the sauce, bring to a boil, then turn off heat and don't cook any longer, but keep warm. The flesh should be tender but not fall apart.

Serve very hot with fresh buttered noodles cooked *al dente*, that is, firm but not crunchy to the teeth.

If your rabbits are young—less than 2 pounds each— don't marinate for more than 2 hours and check on the cooking after 25 minutes.

BARDAQUE BRETONNE
Rabbit-stuffed cabbage with quail

ᔕ ᔕ ᔕ

SERVES 8

This is an old Breton dish made of cabbage leaves stuffed with the meat of a young rabbit and served surrounded with quail and chestnuts. Very welcome at Christmas.

2 medium curly cabbages
1 young rabbit
1¼ pounds fatback cut into
   lardons
6 medium carrots
4 leeks, whites only
2 turnips
2 onions
10 peppercorns
1 bouquet garni (parsley,
   thyme, bay leaf)

dry white wine (Muscadet or
   Gros Plant)
nutmeg
1 piece caul fat or ½-pound
   piece blanched bacon cut into
   wide but thin slices
oil or lard
6–8 quail
salt and pepper
1¼ pounds chestnuts (see
   note)

Take the cabbage apart and remove the veins from the large leaves without tearing them. Blanch leaves in boiling salted water until they are the consistency of thin cloth. Drain and lay out flat on kitchen towels to dry, being careful not to tear.

Remove all the meat from the bones of your rabbit, but reserve the bones. Rinse the fatback lardons and put everything together in a large glass or crockery bowl: the meat, the bones, the fatback, all the vegetables except the cabbage.

Add the peppercorns and the bouquet garni to the white wine and pour it into the bowl, then marinate for 8 hours in the refrigerator.

After 8 hours remove the meat (rabbit and lardons) from the marinade and chop it—not too finely. Place some of the chopped meat in the middle of each cabbage leaf, season with nutmeg, then wrap the leaf around the meat to make a packet about the size of a small orange. Wrap each packet in a piece of caul fat or blanched bacon and tie securely.

Remove the vegetables from the marinade and cut the carrots, turnips, and onions into small dice and the leeks into rounds.

In a large, heavy iron casserole heat 3 tablespoons oil or lard and gently brown the vegetables, then add the bouquet garni, the cabbage packets, and the bones. Pour in the marinade to come halfway up the meat. Cover and simmer over very low heat, watching carefully so that nothing sticks to the bottom.

In another casserole heat more oil or lard and brown the quail. Add salt and pepper, and moisten with a tablespoon of the marinade. Cover and cook over low heat. When the quail have puffed up and released their juices, test them by pricking the skin and wiggling a joint. If the juices run golden rather than red they are done. Turn off heat and set aside to keep warm.

While they are cooking peel the chestnuts, then to remove the inner skins place them on a baking sheet in a medium oven to dry out. When the skin is dry and peels off easily, remove from the oven.

The best way to cook chestnuts is to steam them. A couscous maker is perfect, but you can improvise with a large kettle and a colander. Steam them until they are soft but not mushy. Taste one to test. The time varies radically with the age and size of the nuts.

On a large, deep serving platter arrange cabbage packets in the center, quail and chestnuts around them. Combine the packet-cooking liquid with the quail-cooking liquid, strain, and heat quickly, then spoon some over the food on the serving platter, and serve the rest separately in a sauceboat.

NOTES : If you can't get fresh chestnuts or don't want to bother, you can use canned chestnuts (unsweetened) and purée them with butter. Pipe the purée around the edge of the platter.

Quail is hard to find, and you can substitute squab.

If you prefer to cook the quail in the oven, fill the cavities with thyme, onions, and the giblets, rub the skins with butter, and squeeze half a lemon over each, then put the squeezed lemon half into the cavity. Truss the birds, cover the breasts with strips of blanched bacon, and roast in a 400°F. oven for 40 minutes.

CONCOMBRES EN DARIOLES
Molded cucumber custard

𝒯𝒯𝒯

SERVES 8

3 cucumbers
1 tablespoon butter
6 eggs
⅓ cup crème fraîche
salt and pepper

Peel the cucumbers and cut them into quarters the long way. Scrape out the seeds and core—this is most easily done with a small spoon. Cut the flesh into little pieces and toss into boiling salted water. Cook at a gentle boil for several minutes, until the point of a knife pierces the cucumber but the flesh is still firm. Drain and let cool.

Butter 8 individual soufflé dishes or custard cups.

Preheat oven to 400°F.

Mash the cucumber pieces in a blender or food processor and drain to get rid of the excess liquid. Don't press though —there should be some liquid. Weigh the crushed cucumber. The amounts given above are for 13 ounces.

Beat the eggs as for an omelette with the crème fraîche, then mix in the cucumber. Add salt and pepper. Fill the buttered dishes. Place the individual dishes in a large, shallow, ovenproof dish, then pour in water—hot but not boiling—to come halfway up the sides of the cups. Place in the oven for 18–20 minutes. Watch to see that the water doesn't boil—that would ruin the texture of the finished custard. After 18 minutes test for doneness with the point of a knife. If the knife comes away clean with no liquid the custards are done.

Serve unmolded as an accompaniment for fish, roasts, or braised meats.

MARIE-JO FERRAND

❧❧❧❧❧

Gîte-du-Tourne-Pierre
Challans (Vendée)

A *tourne-pierre* is a bird whose name accurately describes
the way it seeks out its food. The Vendée coasts and marshes
are its habitat. And Marie-Jo, who shares it, has come to
resemble the bird. Slender, roguish, with a walk like a
dancer's, she is the image of enterprising youth. Her *gîte* (an
animal's resting place), built on the edges of the Vendéen
marsh behind a curtain of large trees, which screen it from
the Challans-Soullans road, is her dream made real.

"Mad about cooking," as she says, her instinctive knowledge was nurtured by good teachers: Escoffier and many others. This authority on child welfare had already cultivated her gifts and her imagination so well that no one around her could gainsay her desire to commercialize her talents four or five years ago. Not even her husband, businessman and painter.

Challans! *Canards nantais*, eels, frogs, all the products of the nearby ocean there for her to use. One must taste her lively sautéed shrimp flambéed in bourbon. (When there are no shrimp they are replaced with langoustines.) Or try her clams baked in white wine—the lees of Gros Plant— with green herbs, her eels *maraîchine*, her rabbit grilled over coals and smoked with herbs of Provence tossed into the embers. Her entire repertoire is strongly inspired by local produce, which her original preparation raises above the everyday.

The produce is important. But it's the cooking that makes them special.

Charming Marie-Jo—this year she's going to get started on a garden. The beloved pony who ravaged it has been banished and now the children are grown. Flowers, flowers everywhere. Surely she has a green thumb, too.

BOUQUETS FLAMBÉS AUX WHISKY
Shrimp flamed in bourbon

SERVES 2

1 pound fresh shrimp	salt
2 tablespoons heavy cream	cayenne
juice of ½ lemon	3 tablespoons butter
1 teaspoon tomato paste	½ cup bourbon

This is a recipe that is all done at the last moment and goes very quickly.

Peel the shrimp.

Mix together the cream, lemon juice, tomato paste, and pinches of salt and cayenne.

Heat the butter and drop the shrimp into it. When they have just begun to stiffen sprinkle them with the bourbon and flame. Pour the cream mixture over the shrimp as soon as the fire goes out.

Cook over high heat just until the sauce coats a wooden spoon.

N o t e : Frozen South African lobster tails, 4–5 to a person, can be prepared the same way.

ANGUILLES À LA MARAÎCHINE
Eels with sorrel

SƆ SƆ SƆ

2–3 pounds small, fresh eels	thyme
4 ounces (1 stick) butter	savory
1 pound fresh sorrel (the large	rosemary (fresh if possible)
leaves are good for this	½ cup cream
recipe)	1 egg yolk
1 cup Muscadet	1 lemon
salt and pepper	

Ask your fish store to clean the eels and cut off the heads and the tips of the tails.

Slice the eels into rounds about 3–4 inches long, then heat half the butter in a large frying pan and cook the pieces of eel just to stiffen them.

Trim the stems and large center veins from the sorrel and cut the leaves into pieces with scissors. Place in a saucepan with the rest of the butter and let wilt. Stir until it is a mush.

To the eel pan add enough wine to moisten the eels, stir to mix, then add to the sorrel. Stir in salt and pepper, big pinches of thyme and savory, and a few sprigs of rosemary. Cook, uncovered, at a very low simmer for 15 minutes.

Lightly salt and pepper the cream, then beat in the egg yolk thoroughly, and finally beat in several squirts of lemon juice.

Retrieve the rosemary sprigs from the eel/sorrel pot and add the cream. Reheat carefully without letting it come to a boil, stirring gently (so as not to break up the eels) all the time. It is ready when the sauce coats the spoon.

HOMARDS AUX PETITS LÉGUMES
Lobster with vegetables

𝒮𝒮𝒮

3 lobsters, 2–2½ pounds each
4 ounces (1 stick) butter
½ cup cognac
2 onions
1 clove garlic
2 carrots
heart of 1 bunch of celery
2 leeks

¼ pound mushrooms
1 bouquet garni (parsley, thyme, bay leaf)
1 cup dry white vermouth
2 tablespoons heavy cream
salt and pepper
cayenne

Begin by splitting the live lobsters in half lengthwise. You can do this by inserting a knife in the middle of the chest and severing the spinal column—which is at the front of the lobster. Remove the stomach (it is right behind the head). If you find you can't bear to do this, you can fill a large pot with boiling water and dump the lobsters into it head first. Cook just until they stop moving, then proceed with the recipe.

Melt half the butter in a large iron skillet and cook the lobsters until they turn red. If you have preboiled them, cook for about 3 minutes. Sprinkle with cognac and flame. Let them rest uncovered. Crack the claws and all the joints.

Mince the onions and garlic and cut the other vegetables into a thin, matchstick julienne or chop in a fine dice. Melt the rest of the butter in another skillet and cook the onions and garlic over low heat until they are soft but not browned. Add all the other vegetables and the bouquet garni. When the vegetables have given up their liquid, stir in the vermouth. Bring to a boil and when the liquid evaporates the vegetables should be just right: *al dente*. Add the cream, salt and pepper, and a largish pinch of cayenne, and pour over the lobsters.

Let simmer over low heat for 10 minutes, then taste and correct the seasoning, which should be quite spicy. Serve as is or accompanied by rice Creole (see note).

NOTES: You will probably not have a pan big enough to cook three lobsters, so another way to do this is to remove the claws and tails, which is all you will eat anyway, crack the claws and joints so the seasoning gets into the meat, and proceed. You can use the body of the lobster to make a stock.

Rice Creole is brown rice, about 1½ cups for six, placed in a heavy saucepan and covered with two fingers of water and a little salt. Bring to a boil and cook until the rice is soft, then turn off the heat and set the pot aside, covered, until the rice soaks up the rest of the water. Don't stir. This will take about 1 hour.

LAPIN BARBECUE
Barbecued rabbit

SERVES 4

1 young rabbit, about 2 pounds

salt and pepper

sprigs of aromatic herbs such
as thyme, oregano, marjoram,
rosemary, etc., or several
spoonfuls *herbes de Provence*

1 cup heavy cream

1 tablespoon mustard

salt and pepper

1 lemon

2 tablespoons minced chives

Just before cooking cut the rabbit into pieces—two for each hind leg, two for the breast, and two for each forequarter—one with the leg and one with the saddle on either side. Salt and pepper them and let them sit for a moment. Cook the pieces of rabbit on a barbecue grill, turning them from time to time. They shouldn't brown too quickly if they are going to cook all the way through.

When they begin to take on color, sprinkle the embers —not the rabbit—with the herbs. When the meat is just cooked sprinkle the herbs on the embers again, more abundantly. Serve right off the fire accompanied by the following sauce, which you can prepare while the rabbit is cooking.

Bring the cream and the mustard to a boil and cook until it coats a wooden spoon. Taste, add salt and pepper and a few squirts of lemon juice, then stir in the chives. Either spoon over the cooked rabbit or serve separately in a sauceboat, as you prefer.

SORBET À L'ANANAS FRAIS
Pineapple sherbet

𝒮 𝒮 𝒮

MAKES 1 QUART

1¾ cups sugar
1 medium-size ripe pineapple
juice of 1 lemon
1 egg white

Bring the sugar and ½ cup water to a boil over moderate heat without letting it take on color. When it comes to a boil, reduce the heat slightly, and let it boil for 5 minutes.

While you are making the syrup remove the flesh from the pineapple, making sure no traces of the skin or the fibrous core remain. Put the flesh through a food mill or liquefy in a blender, and then pass through a sieve. Add the lemon juice. This will yield about 2 cups.

When the syrup has boiled for 5 minutes, put the pot into cold water to stop it from cooking, but without chilling it.

Beat the egg white until it is fairly stiff, then continue to beat while you pour in the still-hot syrup in a thin stream. Continue adding the syrup and beating until you have a very fine, soft mousse. This is an Italian meringue. With a wire whisk mix the pineapple purée and the meringue well —but don't beat.

Pour into a flat, metal dish, cover with plastic wrap, and place in the freezer. When it is half-frozen remove from freezer and beat with an electric mixer until it is uniform slush, then return to the freezer to finish freezing. Or freeze in an ice cream freezer according to directions.

MARIE-LOUISE JULIEN

❧❧❧❧❧

Hôtel de la Vieille Poste
Ouroux-en-Morvan (Nièvre)

The dowager peels the vegetables; she is retired. The grand-niece prepares the cheese soufflé; she is beginning. The chef, Marie-Louise Julien, the fifth generation of women chefs at La Vieille Poste, with her well-secured salt-and-pepper chignon, navigates nearby between the tables and the side--board—a captain at her stove.

Ensconced in a corner, it imposes on the kitchen the

pleasant air of a miniature submarine at sea. A pot-au-feu exuding restorative aromas simmers on it surrounded by a pyramid of frying pans and saucepans ready to enter the fray.

"I don't like to use my ovens. I use them only for my tarts and a little pastry in my leisure time," she says. "My customers here like my braised meats with fresh aromatic vegetables gathered from the garden. Since I'm alone I can watch things better on the top of the stove. Frying pans are my preferred implements.

"There are good meats in the Morvan: veal cutlets, which I sauté, then deglaze with cream; kidneys; sautéed slices of beef, well buttered and dressed with garden herbs. People also like my full-flavored omelettes: herb, mushroom, ham. I put everything in. My ham is home-cured, then sautéed and cream is added. It's a regional dish. Taste it."

Prosciutto compares, but barely. She has a special knife to cut it into slices as thin as cigarette paper, as large as a flag, and she explains to all the diners that it is her own "modest ham, made at home."

The Vieille Poste has nothing to do with railway coaches and everything to do with stagecoaches. The courtyard, encircled by stables, recaptures the life of a bygone era. The riders—tourists—fill the little dining room and the coffee bar, which one has to cross to get to it.

"Young people are becoming gourmets," she says, opening up. "Watch how discerningly they compose their meals; how they appreciate good cooking.

"Yes, of course I have specialties. They date from a long time ago and are always based on regional produce.

"My hams"—she wouldn't dare not mention them—"game in winter, although the hunters here have as much of it as I, I prepare it on the weekends. The lakes, the ponds, are full of fish, and frogs swarm in them. In season I have quail, the real ones.

"There is no season for weekends—the snow doesn't stop anyone. The shortest holidays fill the house."

Ouroux-en-Morvan is the heart of the Morvan, so say the tourist brochures. La Vieille Poste is, too.

CUISSES DE GRENOUILLES EN BEIGNETS
Frogs' legs in fritter batter

✑ ✑ ✑

12–16 pairs frogs' legs, depending on the size
⅓ cup vinegar
⅓ cup chopped parsley
pepper
oil for deep frying

Batter
2½ cups flour
1 pinch salt
2 jumbo eggs or 3 large
1 tablespoon oil

Snail butter
6 ounces (1½ sticks) butter
1 clove garlic, pressed
salt and pepper

Soak the frogs' legs in a large shallow dish in the vinegar with the chopped parsley and pepper for 10 minutes, then turn the frogs' legs over and soak on the other side for another 10 minutes. They should not soak for more than 20 minutes.

While they are soaking prepare the fritter batter. Put the flour in a deep bowl and make a well in it. Drop the salt, the whole eggs, and the oil into the well. Blend, adding a little bit of cold water from time to time, using up to 1½ cups water. Beat with a wire whisk until the batter is smooth and fluid. It should be a bit heavier than crêpe batter.

Heat a large pot of oil until it is hot, but not smoking.

Drain and shake dry the frogs' legs without dislodging the specks of parsley clinging to them. One at a time dip them into the batter, and, when they are coated, drop them into the hot oil. They should become golden as they cook.

When they are golden, drain them on absorbent paper and keep them warm while you fry the others. When they are all done, arrange on a serving platter with their ankles together in a teepee and keep warm in a low oven with the door ajar. Over low heat melt the butter with the garlic, salt, and pepper. Keep shaking the pan. It is ready when it feels very hot to your fingers. Don't let it bubble. Pour over the frogs' legs and serve.

CAILLES PAYSANNE
Peasant quail

✐ ✐ ✐

SERVES 4

1 pound bacon, in slab if
  possible
4 ounces (1 stick) butter
4 or 8 quail, depending on how
  plump they are
½ cup dry Madeira

salt and pepper
10 ounces small mushrooms
½ tin *petits grisés* mushrooms,
  drained
4–5 tablespoons heavy cream,
  at room temperature

Cut the bacon into lardons about the diameter of a pencil and blanch it in a pot of boiling water for a few minutes.

Melt 6 tablespoons (¾ stick) butter in a casserole over low to medium heat, and add the drained bacon and the quail. Let them brown, being careful not to burn the butter. Pour in the Madeira, add salt and pepper, cover the casserole, and let cook over very low heat for 30 minutes.

Meanwhile melt the remaining 2 tablespoons butter in a large frying pan and when it is hot stir in both the fresh mushrooms and the canned mushrooms. Cover and cook until they have yielded their excess liquid.

After the quail have cooked for 30 minutes add the drained mushrooms and cook 15 to 20 minutes longer.

Remove the quail to a heated platter to keep warm and add the cream to the cooking juices. Raise the heat and let the mixture boil for 3 minutes. Taste, correct the seasoning, and pour over the quail.

Serve with French-fried potatoes, home-fried potatoes, or even a gratin dauphinois.

NOTES: If you can't get quail, squab can be substituted for this recipe. The cooking time will be the same. If you substitute Rock Cornish game hens, cook longer. But their meat is not really as good and the result won't be quite what Madame Julien had in mind.

And if you can't get *petits grisés* or don't want to spend so much on this dish you can use all regular mushrooms (add about another 2 ounces) or you can substitute any good dried mushroom—inflate them before using, though.

LÉA
BIDAUT

⚜❦⚜❦⚜

La Voûte
Lyon 2ᵉ

There is no one who calls her Léa. A nuance, her title is
Léa of Lyon. One could call her the last of the "mères" from
a line of "mères"—Guy, Filloux, Brazier, etc. She, Léa
Bidaut, says she is without heirs.

"What should I pass on? The tables? The chairs? I
improvise at the moment. My recipe for today, as soon as it
is served, won't be tomorrow's, even with the same produce.
And suppose I were always the same; the times change,
too. I think about fluidity, about astral influences. There are
days when nothing goes right, and others . . ." She is born
under the sign of Leo.

Warm, intelligent, tossing her silver mane, she continues. A gamine, born at Creusot, she began earning her living very young, pursuing only one objective: saving money so that one day she could have a place of her own. She tells of the stages that led to La Voûte in 1943, while she continues with her cooking. She is vast, functional, severe, but she finally drops her reserve. "My chicken in vinegar. I don't even make it at my children's houses on Sundays. It needs too many ingredients I don't have on hand."

Her cooking, which she calls country, is knowingly elaborated. Unquestionably traditional in her bases—refined sauces, purged of flour liaisons in favor of reductions beaten with butter—for her all is craft. Nothing is new. "What is new is the universal interest in gastronomy," she says with a great laugh.

"My gratin Eugénie is very simple"—changing her mind—"no, there is a secret in the base. I won't tell it to you. Come, eat some. Here.

"This rabbit dish is childishly simple. I put everything into it. My poulet aux herbes . . ."

Hungry, I waited. What I wanted were recipes. One had to catch them on the wing. " 'Pioneer's apron,' " but everyone makes that, only one has to . . .

"I don't like cooking that makes you ask if the sugar might not be a scullery boy's error. Even in my haunch of young wild boar I don't use sugar to brown the pineapple. No tricks, nothing slapdash, you see.

"My Canut brains, I make two: the classic and then another which I call Léa's head.

"Really, one has to eat it slowly."

It wasn't the marvelous Chirouble that fuddled me! Astonishing Léa—thank heaven she's so young.

TABLIER DE SAPEUR
"Pioneer's apron"

⟡ ⟡ ⟡

SERVES 4

This is a beef stomach (tripe) cooked for four hours in a court bouillon, coated with bread crumbs, and fried in oil, then eaten with a mayonnaise flavored with a reduction of shallots and tarragon.

1 blanched beef stomach (tripe)	2 turnips
2 onions	salt and pepper
2 carrots	bouquet garni (thyme, parsley,
2 leeks	bay leaf)
3 stalks celery	

Rinse the tripe with cold water and put it into a kettle. Cover with water, bring to a boil, and add all the vegetables, cut in large pieces, the salt and pepper, and the bouquet garni.

Cook at a gentle boil for 4 hours, then let cool in the cooking liquid.

Coating and cooking

flour	1 loaf stale white bread, dried
2 eggs	in the oven, then pulverized
salt and pepper	to make 1½ cups crumbs
1 tablespoon oil	peanut oil for cooking

Lay the tripe out flat on a table and cut into large triangles about 5 inches across the base. Dry them, then put them into a strainer with the flour and toss until they are coated. Keep tossing to get rid of the excess. Beat the eggs with salt and pepper and the tablespoon of oil and dip the floured triangles into the mixture.

Heat two tablespoons of peanut oil in a large frying pan.

Let the egg-coated meat drain, then dip into the fine bread crumbs. Press to make sure the bread crumbs stick and coat, then shake gently to dislodge any excess. Instantly drop into the hot, but not smoking, oil in the frying pan. Cook for 1 minute on one side, then one minute on the other. "Pioneer's apron" does not have to be stiffened or browned —it is already firm. It should remain soft and uncolored by the cooking.

Drain on absorbent paper and serve with special sauce.

Sauce

3 tablespoons butter
2 tablespoons minced shallots
¾ cup dry white wine
10 tarragon leaves, minced
1½ cups well-beaten mayon-
      naise, preferably homemade

In a small saucepan melt the butter and cook the shallots until they are soft but not brown. Add the white wine and tarragon. Cook at a gentle boil until the liquid is reduced to just shallot paste. Add hot to the mayonnaise.

Don't throw away the tripe scraps. Cut them into strips and sauté with onions minced and cooked until golden in oil, then salted, peppered, and moistened with a stream of vinegar at the end of the cooking: tripe lyonnaise.

NOTE: This dish is not for everyone's taste. The tripe has little flavor, although the texture is unique. Don't try serving it to unsuspecting guests.

CUISSOT DE MARCASSIN À L'ANANAS
Haunch of young wild boar with pineapple

ℐ ℐ ℐ

SERVES 8

1 haunch of young wild boar
10 ounces wild boar trimmings
salt and pepper
thyme
bay leaf
parsley
4 shallots, minced
2 cloves garlic marinated in
   1 cup wine vinegar for
   several hours

2 tablespoons minced shallots
8 ounces (2 sticks) butter
1 bottle Beaujolais Villages
1 bouquet garni (thyme, bay
   leaf, parsley)
4 ounces lard
1 cup cognac

Marinate the skinned, boned haunch for 48 hours in the refrigerator in a dry marinade of salt, pepper, thyme, bay leaf, parsley, 4 minced shallots, and the garlic and its wine vinegar. Save the boar bones.

    Collect and save any blood from the haunch in the bowl. Before beginning to cook the meat, make the sauce.

    In a large saucepan over moderate heat soften the 2 tablespoons minced shallots in 1 tablespoon butter. Add the boar trimmings (cut into small pieces) and then the chopped-up bones. Don't let them brown. Stir in the wine, add the bouquet garni, and simmer for 2 hours over low heat. Salt very lightly. Strain, and press on the solids to extract all the juices. Return the strained stock to the stove and reduce it to about 1 cup.

Tie up the haunch to keep it in shape, then dry it. Weigh it—it affects cooking time.

Melt the lard and 3 tablespoons butter in a large heavy casserole over low heat. Brown the haunch on all sides, then sprinkle with the cognac, and flame. Add the reduced stock, cover, and cook over low heat for 20 minutes per pound, turning it occasionally.

Place the haunch on a serving platter and keep warm. Degrease the cooking liquid and add the blood you have kept aside in the bowl. Bring to a boil, then, off the heat, bit by bit beat in the remaining 6 ounces of butter, softened but not melted.

Reheat without letting boil and spoon a little over the haunch. Serve the rest separately in a sauceboat.

Pineapple sautéed in butter
1 large, ripe pineapple
2 ounces (½ stick) butter

Remove the skin and fibrous core from the pineapple. Cut the flesh into 1½-inch cubes. Melt the butter in a frying pan and sauté the pineapple until it is golden. Arrange it around the haunch of boar.

Léa also serves small plates of her celebrated macaroni and cheese (following recipe) with this meal.

NOTE: This dish looks prettier if you remove the strings and slice the boar (which should be pink on the inside) in the kitchen, then re-form it on the serving platter, and surround with the pineapple.

MACARONI AU GRATIN DE LÉA
Léa's macaroni and cheese

♫ ♫ ♫

SERVES 6

2⅔ cups uncooked elbow noodles:
the small ones are better for this dish

Béchamel sauce
2 cups milk
2 generous tablespoons butter
1 generous tablespoon flour
salt and white pepper
2 tablespoons grated Swiss cheese

Cook the macaroni *al dente*, that is to say, firm to the bite
but not crunchy. As soon as it is done, refresh under cold
running water. Drain, then put back into pan over boiling
water to keep warm.

Prepare the béchamel slowly. It has to simmer to
acquire its velvety texture.

Bring the milk to a boil in a small pan and have it
boiling when you add it to the roux. Melt 1 tablespoon
butter in a saucepan, sprinkle in the flour, and stir with a
wooden spoon until the flour starts to take on color and
begins to give off an aroma like baking brioche. Then add
half the boiling milk, stirring constantly with a wire whisk.
When the mixture has thickened, let it simmer for a few
minutes and decide if you need to add any more milk to

obtain a velvety yet light-textured sauce. Add salt and pepper, then continue to simmer for 15–20 minutes.

Place the well-drained macaroni in a gratin dish and cover with the béchamel, thinned or stretched with more milk if necessary. The sauce should barely be level with the top of the macaroni.

Sprinkle with the grated cheese and dot with the remaining tablespoon of butter, then run quickly under the broiler to brown the top.

NOTE: If you want to make this dish ahead of time you can. Both the macaroni and the sauce can be cooked, but they should not be combined until you are ready to serve. Cover the béchamel with plastic wrap or dot the top with butter so it doesn't form a skin, and set aside. If you have cooked the sauce and the macaroni ahead they will be cold, so when you have combined them put them into a moderate (300°F.) oven for about 10 minutes until the sauce is bubbling before running the dish under the broiler.

ANTOINETTE LÉGER

Au Capitaine
Les Sables-d'Olonne (Vendée)

Because her husband sold wine, and as a man of taste he sold good wine, Antoinette decided: for good wine, a good restaurant. We roll up our sleeves.

She knew how to create an enticing setting for her activities, just in front of the marvelous Sables shoals where, as she says, the fish have only to jump out of the ocean into the frying pan.

She is very exacting about the quality of her purchases. "A good restaurant begins at market," she says. She makes her way to the fish market each morning and composes the menu according to what is there. "In my place everything is fresh, not iced or frozen."

As at all the restaurants of her *consoeurs* nothing is cooked in advance, but everything is ready to use: from the minced shallots to the absolutely fresh peeled vegetables, to the orange zests, parsley, and other herbs; in fact, all the ingredients which give originality to her cooking.

A woman alone in charge of a restaurant, no matter how much help she has, has to work in an atmosphere of serenity if she is not going to be driven mad.

It is necessary to give a lot of herself, and to have a taste for giving pleasure if one wants to be a professional cook. Good food is an important oasis in our agitated lives. If our taste is satisfied it alerts all our other senses. The euphoria which comes with good eating is not a vain formula. It is the subtext one hears in her explanation of recipes.

And when Antoinette was asked what her favorite dish is she told us: raw sardines done my way. No, it isn't a recipe, don't write it down. But we did.

Use good, raw sardines. Don't clean them, but wipe them (this rubs off the scales). Eight hours in salt. Run under a faucet, dry, then arrange in a terrine with thyme, bay leaf, sliced onion and carrots, slices of lemon, peppercorns, dry white wine, peanut oil, vinegar. Marination—48 hours in a cool place. With buttered toast and a little glass of cold wine . . . how regal.

HUÎTRES GRATINÉES ANTOINETTE
Antoinette's gratinéed oysters

ℐℐℐ

PER PERSON

6 oysters

2 shallots

1½ ounces mushrooms

1 ounce (¼ stick) butter

¾ cup white wine

¾ cup Pineau de Charentes

salt and pepper

2 tablespoons heavy cream

1 egg yolk

2 tablespoons grated Gruyère
   or Swiss cheese

2 tablespoons blanched
   almonds, ground

Place the oysters in a large pot with a little water and open over high heat. They should poach in their shells. When they are open, remove the oysters from their shells, put the oysters into a bowl, and strain their liquor into the bowl with them. Wash and set aside half of each shell. (If there is no oyster liquor you can pour a little bottled clam juice over the oysters as they sit.)

Mince the shallots and then the mushrooms. Wild mushrooms are preferable, but domestic ones will do fine. In the barely heated butter cook the shallots and mushrooms until they are soft but not brown. Moisten them with the two indicated wines. Salt and pepper lightly. Reduce the mixture over medium heat until it is a wet paste, but no longer really liquid. It will look very nasty, but tastes good.

In another saucepan over low heat beat the cream and the egg yolk, and when the sauce is thick enough to coat a spoon, add the contents of the other pot. Continue to stir, without letting the sauce boil, over very low heat for a few more minutes until the two mixtures have amalgamated. Taste and correct the seasoning.

Arrange the clean oyster shells on a platter that can go under the broiler (a gratin dish is good for this), then place an oyster on each shell and pour the reserved oyster liquor over them. Spoon the sauce over the oysters and sprinkle lightly with the grated cheese and then the ground almonds.

Run under the broiler quickly just to reheat and brown the tops.

SAINT-JACQUES SABLAISES
Sablaises scallops

✍ ✍ ✍

SERVES 4

2 pounds scallops
2 ounces (½ stick) butter
2 ounces minced shallots
¼ cup cognac
3 tablespoons heavy cream

salt and pepper
¼ cup Pineau de Charentes
3 tablespoons bread crumbs
3 tablespoons grated Gruyère
  or Swiss cheese

Fumet

1 pound white fish trimmings
1 bouquet garni (thyme, bay
  leaf, parsley)
1 onion

2 shallots
½ cup white wine
salt and pepper

First put all the ingredients for the fumet into a covered kettle, add 6 cups cold water, and boil for 25 minutes. Let sit for 5 minutes, then strain.

Wash the scallops, put them into the barely tepid fumet, and bring to a boil. Let boil for 2 minutes, then remove from heat.

In a large frying pan melt the butter, then add the shallots and cook until they are soft, but don't let them brown. Add the drained scallops and cook until they stiffen (about 1 minute), stirring constantly. Sprinkle with cognac and flame. When the flame goes out add the cream and salt and pepper. Complete with the wine and return to the boil. As soon as it boils again, remove from heat and distribute the scallops and sauce among clean scallop shells or oven-proof baking dishes or ramekins.

Sprinkle very parsimoniously with the bread crumbs and cheese, and brown quickly under the broiler.

NOTE : In this, as in any seafood (as opposed to fish) recipe, bottled clam juice is a good substitute for making a fish fumet. Substitute it for the trimmings, using ⅓ clam juice to ⅔ water, so for this recipe use 3 cups clam juice.

MOUCLADE VENDÉENNE
Curried mussels

✐ ✐ ✐

SERVES 4

2½ pounds mussels

1 onion

1 level tablespoon curry powder

1 level tablespoon cornstarch

3 tablespoons heavy cream

salt and pepper

Clean the mussels. Don't soak them, but wash them quickly and well and get rid of their beards.

Chop the onion coarsely and add it to 1 cup of water in a large pot. Bring to a boil, drop in the mussels, cover, and let them open over high heat.

Drain the mussels over a bowl and discard any that don't open. Keep them warm without prolonging the cooking. Let the drained liquid rest, then strain it through a tea towel. Return the strained juice to the heat with the curry powder. Dissolve the cornstarch in a little cold water, and when the curry has entirely melted into the mussel juice, add the cornstarch liquid and the cream.

Bring to a boil. Salt and pepper carefully. Add the mussels, reheat rapidly, and serve at once.

ENCORNETS FARCIS AUX FRUITS DE MER
Squid stuffed with seafood

ꙮ ꙮ ꙮ

SERVES 6

6 squid, 6–6½ inches long
12–18 crayfish, or ¾ pound large
shrimp

Stuffing

4 cups mussels	5 ounces prosciutto, chopped
3 tablespoons minced shallots	4 cups scallops
2 ounces mushrooms, chopped	2 tablespoons minced parsley
2 cloves garlic, minced	salt and pepper
2 ounces (½ stick) butter	nutmeg

When you clean the squid, don't tear the pocket. Pull out the horned beak at the tentacles, cut off and reserve the tentacles, and clean the interior well.

Steam the mussels open in a large covered pot. Discard any that don't open. Set aside 12 in their shells and take the rest out of their shells. Strain liquid through cheesecloth and reserve.

Chop the squid tentacles finely, then add the shallots, mushrooms, and garlic. Melt the butter in a large saucepan, then add the above mixture and the prosciutto, and cook for 5 minutes. Off the heat add the mussels and the scallops (if they are large, halve or even quarter the scallops). Save any juice from the scallops and strain into the strained mussel liquor.

Add the parsley to this stuffing, then salt, pepper, and nutmeg. Fill the squid with it and sew the opening of the pocket closed.

Cooking sauce

3 tablespoons lard or oil

3 onions, minced

3 tablespoons tomato paste

1 cup white wine

1 sprig thyme

salt and pepper

cayenne

½ cup cognac, warmed

2 tablespoons heavy cream

½ cup Pineau de Charentes

5 ounces (1¼ sticks) butter at
  room temperature

In a large, heavy-bottomed saucepan or casserole heat the lard or oil and cook the onions until they are soft, but don't let them brown. Add the tomato paste, the white wine, several spoonfuls of the mussel and scallop juices (or use bottled clam juice), the thyme, and salt, pepper, and a pinch of cayenne. Arrange the stuffed squid in the sauce so they don't overlap, and simmer for 25 minutes.

While they are cooking, clean the crayfish or shrimp and cook them in a little oil until they are stiff. Salt and pepper vigorously, then sprinkle with the warmed cognac and flame.

With a slotted spoon remove the cooked squid to a serving bowl and keep warm. Add the crayfish to the sauce, bring to a boil, then immediately remove the crayfish and arrange them around the squid. Stir the cream and the Pineau into the sauce, then strain it and return to the heat. Reduce over high heat, if it is too thin. Off the heat beat in the butter, piece by piece, to bind the sauce. Add the mussels in their shells and pour the sauce over the squid and crayfish. Serve hot.

BAR AU BEURRE BLANC
OU AU BEURRE ROUGE
Bass with red- or white-wine butter sauce

✍ ✍ ✍

BUTTER FOR 6 SERVINGS

When Antoinette has a big fish such as a fine bass, she cuts off the head and steams the flesh. The skin is removed at the table and the fish accompanied with a beurre nantais.

4 tablespoons minced shallots	12 ounces (3 sticks) butter
¾ cup wine vinegar	salt and pepper
¼ cup white wine (such as Muscadet or Gros Plant)	

Over moderate heat, reduce the shallots with the vinegar and wine until the mixture is nothing but a shallot paste.

In another pot heat 4 tablespoons water over moderate heat and add the butter about a tablespoon at a time, stirring constantly with a wire whisk. It is important that it not boil.

Add the shallot paste a spoonful at a time to the melted butter, stirring constantly with a wire whisk. Again, this should not boil, and the sauce should thicken and rise, so it is about the consistency of hollandaise.

Add salt and pepper to taste.

Beurre rouge
Make it exactly the same way but with a red wine such as a Gigondas or Côtes de Rhône.

NOTE: This sauce must be served immediately. If it sits it will turn back to a butter consistency. Should this happen, beat a little in a cold bowl, then gradually beat the rest back in to obtain the desired consistency again.

SIMONE LEMAIRE

❦❦❦

Le Tourne-Bride
Le Pin-au-Haras, Exmes (Orne)

Self-confidence is the spirit that radiates from Simone Lemaire when she, captivating Normande, welcomes us.

Her smile is as open as everything about her. But don't think it's formula. She supervises her establishment and is tough about it.

With her, one immediately gets to the core of the subject.

Good dining begins with a hot plate; alimentary hygiene is the origin of the changes in today's cooking. Gently, quietly, she modified the use of fats, of sauces weighed down with too-elaborate bases, of bindings, even the general order of a meal.

Woman is born a cook, man becomes one. She used as proof the students who have become her aides. But they are all still far from the Simone who at twelve years old, for the first communion of one of the children of the household staff, prepared a luncheon for twenty-five.

Her grandmother, with seven children, organized meals which have left her with more than memories.

The palate educates itself. It is a luxury to be able to appreciate, to have for comparison the best preparations, the best wines; to have heard the comments of connoisseurs.

"One can't have good cooking without good things—Curnonsky," she says, citing her authority.

The marketing is exclusively hers. She wants to choose everything. She knows her needs and is so skillful at buying that after a weekend there is no fresh food left over. She also has her kitchen garden with beds of various salad greens going in all different seasons and an abundance of herbs. If she has a bed of curly parsley to decorate a platter, her bed of Italian parsley, the real kind, is even larger.

She also has a cold, dark pond which is her personal fish preserve, fed by running water, for trout and shrimp.

Her menu is rich in surprises of quality. When asked what women tend to order the answer is "most often shrimp or quail."

"Jealous of my recipes? Never. They protect themselves. It is a known fact that ten different hands making the same recipe will turn out ten different dishes. And then, everything is always new. In life what counts lasts."

TURBOTIN DUGLÉRÉ
Flounder with tomato and cream sauce

𝒮𝒮𝒮

SERVES 6

6 flounders, about 1 pound each

Fumet

1½ pounds white fish   5 peppercorns
   trimmings   1 sprig thyme
3 leeks, white parts only   1 bottle dry white wine
2 carrots   1 bunch chervil
6–8 sprigs parsley

Sauce

4 ounces (1 stick) butter
4 shallots, minced
¾ cup crème fraîche
2 egg yolks
3 tomatoes, peeled, seeded, and
   chopped

The fumet should be used cold, so make it the day before.

In a kettle combine the fish trimmings—backs, heads, etc.—with the other fumet ingredients and 4 cups of water. Cook at a gentle boil for 25–30 minutes. Let cool, then strain. Remove the leeks and the carrots; purée them and set them aside. Discard the rest of the strained-out material. Let the fumet cool completely.

Arrange the flounders in a large, deep pan (a *sautoir*

would be perfect) so that they don't overlap, and pour the cold fumet over them. Add enough water so that the fish are completely covered.

Bring to just a wrinkle of a boil and cook for 6 minutes. Remove from the heat and let cool uncovered. Skin the fish and remove the bones on the side, but not the spine or the head. Arrange the fish on a serving platter, moisten with the strained fumet, cover with foil, and set aside to wait over a pot of hot water.

Over high heat, at a rolling boil, reduce 4 cups of the fumet to 1 cup. In a large saucepan melt the butter, then add the minced shallots. Cook over low heat until the shallots are soft, but don't let them brown. Add the reserved carrot and leek purée, the reduced fumet, and the crème fraîche. Let boil for 10 minutes, until the sauce coats a wooden spoon.

In a small bowl beat the egg yolks just to mix, then add the tomatoes.

Pour a little of the hot sauce into the egg mixture, beating as you add, then when the eggs are warm, off the heat add them to the rest of the sauce in the pot. Heat rapidly without letting it boil, stirring constantly. Correct the seasoning. Drain the fish of the fumet you spooned over them (they should still be nice and warm), pour the sauce over them, and serve.

NOTE: You can also make this dish with flounder fillets. Cook in exactly the same way but shorten the cooking time to about 3 minutes. But when you are removing them from the cooking liquid after poaching use two spatulas, as they are brittle and will crack apart if you aren't careful.

CAILLES AU GENIÈVRE
Quail with juniper

ℐℐℐ

SERVES 6

2 tablespoons butter
2 tablespoons oil
salt and pepper
6 quail
12 slices bacon

5 tablespoons gin
2 teaspoons juniper berries,
   crushed
1 cup heavy cream

Heat the butter and oil in a cast iron casserole. Salt and pepper the insides of the quail, then brown them on all sides in the butter and oil. While they are browning, blanch the bacon in boiling water, and when the quail are ready, put two slices of bacon over the breast of each. This is called barding. Cover the casserole and cook over low heat for 30–35 minutes.

Remove all fat from the cooking juices, then heat the gin and sprinkle it over the quail in the remaining juices. Set afire and shake the pot until the fire goes out. When it does, remove the quail from the pot and keep them warm. Add the crushed juniper berries and the cream to the pan juices.

Bring to a boil, stirring constantly. Be sure to scrape up and blend in any bits stuck to the bottom of the pot. The sauce is ready when it coats a wooden spoon. Correct the seasoning.

Remove the bacon from the quail breasts, mince it, and add it to the sauce. Keep warm over very low heat. When you are ready to serve, bring to a boil again quickly and serve very hot in a sauceboat.

COEUR DE FILET POÊLÉ À L'ORANGE
Pan-cooked fillet of beef with orange

⫷ ⫷ ⫷

SERVES 4

2 oranges	6 ounces (1½ sticks) butter
¼ cup Curaçao	4 slices fillet of beef, each about
salt and pepper	½ pound
4 slices marrow bone	parsley

Remove the zest from the oranges and slice it into filaments as small as possible. Blanch until you can crush them between your fingers. Rinse under cold water and dry. Set the pieces aside in a bowl with the Curaçao.

Squeeze the juice from the oranges and set it aside.

Salt and pepper the marrow and wrap each piece of bone in aluminum foil. Drop the foil-wrapped packages into a pot of barely simmering water, then turn the heat off and let them sit and wait.

In a frying pan large enough so that the pieces of fillet won't overlap, melt 4 tablespoons butter. When it is melted, arrange the fillet slices in the pan. Over fairly high heat sear first one side, then the other.

Just before the beef is cooked to the point you desire—rare, medium, etc.—remove it to a hot serving platter. The meat will finish its cooking from contact with the external heat.

Discard all the fat in the frying pan, but carefully conserve any juices or stuck-on bits. Deglaze with the orange juice and 2 tablespoons of water over high heat, using the back of a fork to help you scratch up any bits that might stick.

While the sauce is at a high boil, add the zest and the Curaçao, and then the remaining butter (1 stick), cut up into bits. Remove from the heat and shake the pan. Also use the fork to stir the bits of butter and help them melt in the rapidly boiling liquid. This will bind and smooth the sauce. Correct the seasoning and pour over the meat. Decorate with the marrow removed from the bones and the parsley. Serve immediately.

Serve with pommes Darphin (following recipe).

POMMES DARPHIN
Potato cake

𝒟 𝒟 𝒟

1¾ pounds (6 smallish) potatoes
salt and pepper
4 ounces (1 stick) butter
2 tablespoons oil or goose fat

Very important to the success of this potato cake is the quality of the frying pan. It must be perfectly slippery—preferably nonstick.

Peel the potatoes and grate on the largest holes of your grater, or cut them into matchsticks. Dry them by pressing them with a dish towel. Salt and pepper them very lightly.

As you are doing this you should be melting the butter with oil or goose fat. Immediately toss the potatoes into the pan (otherwise they will darken). Press them against the bottom of the pan, making sure the cake is the same thickness all over. Cook them over moderate heat, shaking the pan from time to time until the bottom of the cake is crusty and golden. Then turn the cake over and brown the other side.

If you can't serve immediately, turn the cake out onto a serving platter and keep hot. This should be served very hot.

NOTE: One way to help assure success is to use a nonstick 8-inch pan and cook this recipe in two batches. Grate half the potatoes and cook them, then keep that cake warm while you grate and cook the other half.

OMELETTE SOUFFLÉE
Dessert omelette

✎✎✎

SERVES 2

This omelette is for only two people. If you want to serve this for a party, make several rather than multiplying the recipe. A very slippery or nonstick pan is essential for this.

3 eggs	2 tablespoons butter
3 tablespoons sugar	2 tablespoons Grand Marnier
juice of 1 lemon	2 tablespoons cognac

Preheat the oven to 550°F. You will finish cooking this dish there.

Separate the eggs. Beat the yolks with the sugar and several squirts of lemon juice until they are light-colored and frothy.

Beat the whites into stiff peaks, then fold them carefully into the yolks, lifting the yolk mixture up from the bottom with each fold.

Melt the butter in a nonstick frying pan. When it is melted, pour in the egg mixture and smooth the surface. Cook over moderate heat until the bottom has become golden.

Put the pan into the hot oven. The omelette will inflate. Don't let it brown, but when the top surface is golden (a few minutes) remove from the oven and slide it onto a serving plate, folding it over on itself as you slide.

Mix the liqueurs together, heat, and at the table flame and sprinkle on the omelette. When flames go out, serve the dessert.

SORBET AUX PAMPLEMOUSSES ROSES
Pink grapefruit sherbet

$\mathscr{D}\mathscr{D}\mathscr{D}$

3 grapefruits
2½ cups sugar
2 tablespoons strawberry syrup
(see note)

Remove the zest from the grapefruits and cut the strips into pieces as tiny as possible. Blanch in 1 quart of boiling water until you can crush the pieces between your fingers.

Prepare the sugar syrup. Put the sugar into 3 cups of water. Add the drained zest, bring to a boil over moderate heat, and boil until it has cooked down to about 2 cups. Remove from heat.

Squeeze the juice from the grapefruits and strain. You should have about 2 cups. Add the strawberry syrup, then pour into the sugar syrup, mix, and let cool.

Freeze in an ice cream maker according to directions, or pour into a metal bowl and still-freeze in your freezer. This works perfectly with this heavy sherbet.

N O T E : Strawberry syrup is available at fancy specialty stores, but if you can't find it you can drain off the syrup from frozen strawberries and use that.

CHRISTIANE MASSIA

❧❧❧❧

L'Aquitaine
Paris 15ᵉ

Here, everything is creative, from the menu to the decor.
From the maritime southwest, Christiane Massia, using her
imagination and her talent, introduces us to rillettes of eel,
a stew of tuna with new vegetables, a brandade soufflé,
scallops on a bed of leeks. Shad and lamprey have their turn
when they are in season. Nothing is stored on ice, nothing
frozen goes into her cooking.

But don't think that the Aquitaine menu will be exclusively reserved for fish. Christiane also makes good use of the Landes chickens, of the Chalosse beef. Normandy is to the southwest, and there they have meats grilled on embers of vine shoots and those meats have become rivals to the daubes which have done so much for the renown of the Marché.

There is always the famous green salad which includes the skin of the grilled ducks, or duck with cèpes, fresh duck foie gras en papillottes, or game in season. And, for most, a revelation: Gironde caviar. Yes, there are sturgeons in her estuary.

Another revelation: the vegetables which are so often neglected, at home as well as in restaurants. Each meal includes some of the better-known, more-or-less forgotten ones —cooked whole or in a gratinéed purée. When you have tasted the purée of Jerusalem artichokes, a vegetable with bad memories for so many generations, you will understand that you have never really tasted it before. And the purée of Boston lettuce—would you recognize it?

All the raw materials come from around Mont-de-Marsan. Products of the earth, grown on farms, have flavors forgotten since the artificial fertilizers of industrial farming altered them.

L'Aquitaine, a restaurant made from a tumbledown resort, is not the least of the Massias' success: the tables and the comfortable chairs are as much testimony to a refined taste as are the Baccarat glasses.

But the loveliest surprise in the restaurant is Christiane. One expects her to be of a weight to equal her achievements; one imagines her a solid Juno with cheeks flushed from the stove . . . and she is nothing like that. She appeared—a young, blonde, slender, tiny woman with a shy smile soliciting your indulgence, but her humorous eyes are ready to gather in your compliments. You ask yourself: Is she being ironic when she asks if you appreciated her fresh-from-the-oven, still-warm madeleines and her preserves? These reminders of a grandmother's desserts have melted us, dear Christiane.

SAINT-JACQUES AUX POIREAUX
Scallops and leeks

3 pounds scallops	salt and pepper
8 medium leeks	cayenne
1 ounce (¼ stick) butter	nutmeg
⅔ cup crème fraîche	

Wash and dry the scallops. This dish is prettier if you use scallops and leeks with the same diameter. So if you have to use sea scallops and have small leeks halve or quarter the scallops. Clean the leeks well. Use only the whites of the leeks and tie them together into little bundles, then cook in boiling salted water until they are tender but not mushy. Remove from the water and refresh immediately under cold running water. Drain them well and then dry, pressing to get as much liquid as possible out of them. Cut into rounds about ½ inch long or about the same size as the scallops.

Butter individual ovenproof dishes or scallop shells. Mix the leeks and scallops together and divide them among the dishes. If there is any coral (the red part) put it on top. To the crème fraîche add salt, pepper, a dash of cayenne, and one grating of nutmeg. Taste; it shouldn't be bland. Spoon generously over the leeks and scallops, then bake in a 400°F. oven for 13–15 minutes.

TURBOTINS AU SAUTERNES
Flounder with sauterne

ℐ ℐ ℐ

2 ounces (½ stick) butter
4 shallots, minced
2 flounders, about 1½–1¾
   pounds each
salt and pepper

½ cup good sauterne
½ cup heavy cream
cayenne
lemon wedges

Preheat the oven to 400°F.

Using all the butter, lavishly butter a large, long oven-proof dish and sprinkle the bottom with the minced shallots.

Arrange the flounders, white skin down, on the bed of shallots so they don't overlap.

Salt and pepper them and sprinkle with sauterne. Spoon the cream over the top, salt and pepper again, and add a pinch of cayenne. Cover with a piece of aluminum foil.

Place in the preheated oven for 10 minutes, then turn the heat down to 350°F. so the liquid doesn't boil violently. Cook for about another 20 minutes at the lower heat.

Remove the fish from the oven, fillet them, and serve on a hot platter. Put the sauce through a fine sieve, then spoon some over the fish, and serve the rest in a sauceboat with some lemon wedges on the table.

Accompany with gratinéed purée of leeks (the following recipe).

NOTE: This dish can be made just as well and more conveniently with an equivalent weight of flounder fillets, but reduce cooking time by about half.

PURÉE DE POIREAUX GRATINÉE
Gratinéed purée of leeks

2¼ pounds leeks (4 large or
  6 small)
2 ounces (½ stick) butter
salt and pepper

2 egg yolks
⅔ cup heavy cream
4 tablespoons grated Gruyère
  or Swiss cheese

Peel the leeks, including about an inch or so of the green. Cut them into ½-inch pieces. Wash them very carefully, dry them, then sauté them in the butter until they are soft. Add water to come just to the top of the leeks. Cook, uncovered, until the water has evaporated.

Put the leeks through a food mill or purée in a food processor. If they still seem too liquid, put them back into the pot over high heat until the excess evaporates. Add salt and pepper.

Mix the yolks with the cream and a tablespoon of the grated cheese and stir into the leeks. Turn the mixture into a shallow, heatproof dish and sprinkle with the rest of the cheese. Put under the broiler, on the rack farthest from the heat, for 10–15 minutes.

NAVARIN DE THON AUX LÉGUMES NOUVEAUX
Tuna cooked with new vegetables

ᑯ ᑯ ᑯ

SERVES 4

½ pound shelled peas
4 ounces very tiny green beans
6 ounces (1½ sticks) butter
8 little new carrots
8 small white onions
4 small round turnips
1 bouquet garni (parsley,
    thyme, ½ bay leaf)

2 cloves garlic, unpeeled
2 pounds fresh tuna fish
salt and pepper
cayenne
chives, cut with scissors

For this recipe choose the smallest, youngest vegetables you can find, so they can remain whole.

Cook the peas and beans separately in boiling, salted water. They should stay green and crunchy. Drain and set aside.

In an iron casserole melt half the butter, then add the carrots, onions, and turnips and let them "sweat." Add the bouquet garni and garlic cloves, and cook over very low heat for 10 minutes. Add the tuna, cover with water, raise the heat a little, and cook at the verge of a simmer, so the fish doesn't move around, for about 20 minutes. Add salt and pepper and a pinch of cayenne. When the cooking is finished (the fish should be stiff) add the peas, green beans, and the rest of the butter. Swirl the casserole from front to back to spread out the butter, which will bind the sauce. Don't stir with a spoon or you will break up the fish. Remove garlic and bay leaf.

Transfer everything immediately and carefully to a hot bowl and sprinkle with the chopped chives. Serve instantly.

BOEUF EN DAUBE DE CHALOSSE
Beef stew

𝒮𝒮𝒮

SERVES 8 TO 10

6½ pounds beef round
1 pound ham
4 tablespoons goose fat or lard
4½ pounds onions, minced
2 tablespoons Armagnac
4½ pounds carrots, sliced
5 cloves garlic, crushed
3 veal bones

1 bouquet garni (thyme,
   parsley, bay leaf)
2 bottles strong red wine
   (Cahors or Gigondas)
salt and pepper
1 loaf good white bread
1 clove garlic, halved

Cut the beef into large stewing pieces and dice the ham. Melt the goose fat or lard in a large iron casserole and brown the beef, the ham, and the minced onions. When they are browned and hot, sprinkle with the Armagnac and flame.

Add the carrots, the 5 cloves crushed garlic, the bones, and the bouquet garni, and pour in the wine. Mix well; add salt and pepper. Cover and cook over very low heat for 2½ hours or in a low (250°F.) oven. Whether in the oven or on top of the stove the liquid should be only at the merest simmer.

Several minutes before serving, toast as many slices of bread as you have diners, rub each piece well with garlic, and arrange on top of the stew in a serving bowl.

The longer the daube is cooked in large quantity, the better it will be. So if you will only be four for dinner, cook the quantity indicated above, and put the rest in sealed jars. Cook for 2 hours in a preserving kettle (or in a pressure cooker, following directions). Using this method, you can keep the stew for several months in a cool, dark place. Or just cook as directed above and freeze the extra.

NOTE: In summer you can make the same daube and serve it cold by adding a calf's foot at the beginning of the cooking and strengthening the seasoning and aromatic vegetables. Let cook an hour longer—the meat should be falling apart.

Divide into individual bowls or into a glass ring mold or deep dish. Let cool, then refrigerate. The gelatin should set in 2 hours.

CHOU FARCI DU MARCHÉ
Stuffed cabbage

SS SS SS

SERVES 6 TO 8

1 large curly cabbage

Stuffing

10 ounces ham, trimmed of fat, but save the fat	1 clove garlic
2 onions	1 thick slice stale white bread, crumbled
½ pound fatback	1 egg
12 ounces pork shoulder	salt and pepper

Cooking

1 pound blanched bacon
1 small pig's knuckle
4 fresh pork sausages
4 carrots
4 leeks

Chop together the ham, onions, fatback, pork, and garlic. Add the bread, then break in the egg. Knead together with your hands. Salt very lightly because of the bacon, but add pepper generously. Let the stuffing rest.

Pull off the cabbage leaves one by one and cook them in boiling water just until they are soft. Cut the ribs out of the big leaves without tearing the leaves. Spread cheesecloth out in a large bowl (this is easier if you dampen the cloth first) and arrange the largest cabbage leaves so that they overlap and form a bowl. There should be no spaces.

Now stuff the other, smaller leaves one by one, roll them up, and arrange them in the bowl of large leaves. Finish with the little white heart of the cabbage. Wrap the cheese-cloth around tightly, bringing up the sides and tying them together with string at the top. Be very careful with this operation because its purpose is to keep the cabbage in place.

Rinse the bacon, pig's knuckle, and sausages. Then place them in a large, heavy kettle with 12 cups water. Bring to a boil, skim, and let cook 45 minutes. Meanwhile tie the carrots and leeks together so they don't come apart.

After 45 minutes, lower the heat and add the cabbage bundle, carrots, and leeks. Simmer gently for 2½ hours. Don't add salt.

To serve, drain the cabbage bundle well, remove the cloth, and cut into slices. Arrange on a serving platter surrounded by the cooked vegetables and the meat cut into eating pieces. Accompany with condiments such as mustard and cornichons, etc., and also give each person a small cup of well-degreased stock.

Remember—all the cured meat in this dish gives off a lot of salt, so don't add any until you taste.

COLETTE MAUDONNET

Aux Naulets d'Anjou
Gennes (Maine-et-Loire)

Les Naulets d'Anjou are porcelain crèche figures created by Paul Maudonnet (Naulet means Noël). They are the symbol of an inn solidly seated on the summit of a hillside overlooking a valley so rich in details that one hesitates to step over the threshold of the door.

A young woman, tall, svelte, distinguished, smilingly welcomes us and immediately communication is established.

"How did I begin cooking? It was eight years ago that my husband, an engineer in an industrial town in the east, decided to come and find us a place in this beautiful Anjou country where he had gone to school.

"This was a small hotel, and would have assured us the wherewithal to live 'dreamily.' But the hotel licenser, to distribute his manna, insisted on a hotel-restaurant. Why not?

"In my restaurant people like the well-prepared vegetables, and the variety of my menus on which my Jacou-le-Croquant chicken, my Englishwoman's tart, and river and ocean fish alternate in season.

"With the help of one of my daughters I have had the time to start, in the basement and the garden apartment, a little school to teach crafts: pottery, woodwork, weaving, design, painting, and so on, all vouched for by the professors of the Anjou school of arts and sciences.

"This activity, my preparation for a second career, 'for retirement,' met with everyone's satisfaction. The young people came. Summer is a very busy season here, as are all vacation times.

"I have to find other things to do for the off season. I'm thinking about it."

She'll find them, this astounding Colette.

SALADE GÉNOISE
Génoise salad

⁐⁐⁐

SERVES 6

4 medium artichokes
lemons
10 ounces green beans
10 ounces small mushrooms
4 tomatoes
4 hard-boiled eggs
salad greens
6 ounces small black olives
   (preferably oil-cured)

olive oil
cider vinegar
2 white onions or 1 yellow,
   minced
4 tablespoons chopped mixed
   fresh herbs or chervil
salt and pepper

Pull the leaves off the raw artichokes and cook the bottoms in lots of salted boiling water until they can be pierced easily with the point of a small knife. Scrape out the prickly chokes and cut the bottoms into 6 or 8 wedges. Squeeze lemon juice onto the pieces.

Cook the green beans until they are *al dente*, that is, they should remain firm to the teeth. Cook in a large pot of salted water so they remain green.

Cut the earth-covered ends off the mushroom stems. Wash rapidly in water to which lemon juice has been added, then dry the mushrooms and cut them into quarters, and squeeze more lemon juice over them to keep them white.

Cut the tomatoes and hard-boiled eggs into quarters. Cover the bottom of a large plate with various salad greens, arrange the rest of the ingredients over it according to your fancy, and then scatter on the olives. Set aside in the refrigerator.

Prepare a vinaigrette of four-fifths olive oil to one-fifth cider vinegar, the minced onion, the herbs, and salt and pepper. Let the dressing stand and steep until you are ready to serve.

POULE JACOU-LE-CROQUANT
SAUCE DE SORGES
Jacou-le-Croquant chicken with Sorges sauce

𝒮𝒮𝒮

SERVES 6 TO 8

1 plump chicken, about 3½–4
  pounds
1 pound stale bread, torn into
  pieces
2 cloves garlic, crushed
3 tablespoons chopped parsley

6 ounces goose cracklings
6 ounces ham fat, cut into small
  pieces
salt and pepper
nutmeg
3 eggs

Choose a good, meaty chicken, not one with a lot of fat. In a large bowl combine the bread pieces, garlic, parsley, goose cracklings, and ham fat. Add salt, pepper, and nutmeg. Break the eggs into this mixture and stir them in. Put this rough-looking stuffing into the cavity of the chicken and sew up all the openings. Be careful that the stuffing isn't compressed and squeezed out. It will expand during the cooking and could burst the chicken.

Stock

1 head celery
4 leeks
1 pound carrots
1 large turnip

2 onions
1 bouquet garni (parsley,
  thyme, bay leaf)
chervil, cut with scissors

Plunge the chicken into a kettle of cold water, bring to a boil, and skim. Let cook at barely a simmer for 1½ hours.

Meanwhile, prepare the celery, leeks, and carrots by tying them into neat bundles. Add the vegetables and the bouquet garni to the kettle after the chicken has cooked for 1½ hours, and cook for 30 more minutes.

Strain and degrease the stock by pouring it through a wet, then wrung-out, doubled-over tea towel. Serve the stock in cups with a teaspoon of chervil in each.

Carve the chicken and arrange. it, without the carcass, on a serving platter. Slice the stuffing, remove the string from the vegetables, and arrange both on the serving platter. Serve with Sorges sauce (see below).

"My Sorges sauce"

1 lemon	8 ounces unflavored yogurt,
chervil	at room temperature
tarragon	2 tablespoons oil
chives	salt and pepper
2 eggs	

Grate the lemon rind and squeeze the juice. Set both aside.

Chop the herbs very finely. Don't use too much tarragon.

Boil the eggs for 3½–4 minutes, or so that you can remove the yolks in one piece and mash the whites into the sauce at the end. They should not be absolutely hard.

Put the very hot yolks into a bowl with the lemon rind and a few spoonfuls of lemon juice. Whisk to lighten the yolks and add, as you beat, a little yogurt, then a little oil and lemon juice, alternating until the sauce is smooth and silky.

Add salt and pepper to taste. Mash the whites with a fork, then add them, with the chopped herbs.

NOTES: If you haven't preserved a goose lately and don't have cracklings on hand, you can substitute the liver, heart, and gizzard of the chicken, chopped very fine and cooked until almost hard in chicken fat.

If you are the cook and you want to serve the chicken bouillon as a first course, you can keep the chicken warm in the oven while you have your first course. Spoon a few tablespoons of the bouillon over it first. The Sorges sauce can be kept in the oven, too, if the yogurt was at room temperature when you added it.

BEIGNETS DE COURGETTES À L'ORIENTALE
Zucchini fritters

𝒮𝒮𝒮

SERVES 6

These fritters go well with roast or broiled meat and also make a nice hot hors d'oeuvre.

2¼ pounds small zucchini	salt and pepper
3 medium onions	nutmeg
2 cloves garlic	1 teaspoon baking powder
1 bunch parsley	flour
3 eggs	oil for frying

Wash and dry the unpeeled zucchini and put them through a meat grinder with the onions, garlic, and parsley—or use a food processor. Let the purée drain through a strainer for about 4 hours.

Put the mixture into a bowl and add the eggs, salt, pepper, and nutmeg. Mix well and taste. It should be very highly seasoned. Stir in the baking powder and then start adding flour, a little at a time. As you add the flour knead with your hand until the paste is a consistency so that you can form it into a ball and place it on a fork and it will hold its shape but remain soft.

Heat about 2–3 inches of oil in a large frying pan.

Form all of the mixture into smallish balls and drop them (as many as will fit without crowding at one time) into the hot oil. Let them cook slowly, regulating the heat so that they brown evenly. They are done when they are a lovely golden color all over.

Drain on absorbent paper. Serve hot.

SOUFFLÉ MISTRAL
Zucchini soufflé

♫ ♫ ♫

SERVES 8

2¼ pounds zucchini
3 ounces (¾ stick) butter
1 pound white onions, chopped
7 ounces cooked ham in thick
  slices
1 tablespoon olive oil
4 tomatoes, peeled, seeded, and
  chopped

3 eggs
salt and pepper
4 tablespoons bread crumbs
4 tablespoons grated Gruyère
  or Swiss cheese

Preheat oven to 350°F.

Peel the zucchini and chop coarsely. In a heavy skillet melt 4 tablespoons butter and cook the zucchini with the onions until they are soft but not brown, then turn up the heat to evaporate any excess liquid so that only butter is left.

Dice the ham and in another pot cook it in the olive oil until the meat is stiff, but don't let it brown. Add the tomatoes and continue cooking until the mixture has become a paste. Combine with the zucchini and onions and put through the largest blade of a food mill or chop coarsely in a food processor. What you want is a rough purée. Add the eggs, then salt and pepper, and spoon into eight buttered individual ramekins. Mix the bread crumbs and the cheese and sprinkle the top of each ramekin with the mixture. Dot with the remaining 2 tablespoons of butter and bake for 8–10 minutes without letting it boil.

Serve hot, but not burning, in the ramekins as a first course, or unmold to accompany a red or white meat.

MOUSSE AU CHOCOLAT
Chocolate mousse

ℐ ℐ ℐ

SERVES 6

9 ounces bittersweet chocolate, as bitter as possible
1 tablespoon very strong coffee
2 ounces (½ stick) butter
3 eggs
8 tablespoons extra-fine sugar
1 tablespoon Grand Marnier (optional)
⅔ cup crème fraîche or heavy cream

Break the chocolate into pieces and put in the top of a double boiler. Moisten it with the coffee and place it over very hot but not boiling water. Melt without stirring until the chocolate is just soft. Off the heat stir in the butter with a wooden spoon.

Separate the eggs. In a bowl beat the yolks with the sugar until they are light and fluffy. Add the chocolate and the Grand Marnier if you like the taste. (You don't have to add any additional flavoring for this mousse, but if you wanted to you could add ½ teaspoon of vanilla instead of the liqueur.)

Beat the cream until it forms soft peaks. If you are using crème fraîche you may have to lighten it with 1 or 2 spoonfuls of ice water. Beat the egg whites until they form soft peaks, too, then very carefully combine the beaten whites with the beaten cream, and fold into the cooled chocolate.

Put into the refrigerator for at least 3 hours. The colder this mousse becomes the more delicate it will be.

The classic accompaniment for this dish is almond tuiles, tea biscuits, or gaufrettes, but a warm brioche is equally fine.

TARTE À L'ANGLAISE
Englishwoman's tart

≪ ≪ ≪

This is an upside-down tart. The fruit is under the crust.
Turn it over to serve, or, if you make it in a quiche dish,
serve just as it comes from the oven, still warm.

3 cups brown sugar
2¼ pounds medium-size apples
  (4–5)
1 lemon
⅔ cup flour

4 ounces (1 stick) butter,
  softened
1½ cups coarsely ground
  blanched almonds
2 cups thick crème fraîche

Sprinkle about 2½ cups of the sugar in a layer ½ inch thick
in the bottom of the pie plate.

Peel and core the apples and cut into quarters. Sprinkle
with lemon juice and arrange rounded side down on top of
the sugar.

With your hands mix together the rest of the sugar, the
flour, the softened butter, and the almonds. The mixture
will be quite coarse; don't try to smooth it out or it will
toughen. Spread it over the apples, covering the whole
surface. Even it without pressing.

Preheat oven to 450°F.

Place the pan over very low heat so the bottom gets hot
and the sugar melts but doesn't caramelize. It will do that
in the oven.

Place in the preheated oven for 30 minutes, watching the color to see that it doesn't get too dark. When the point of a knife pierces the apples easily, the tart is done.

Serve upside-down, warm, with a pot of thick crème fraîche.

HUGUETTE
MELIET

⚜⚜⚜⚜⚜

Moulin de Poüy
Eauze (Gers)

Surprise! Le Moulin de Poüy is a municipal recreation center, an oasis encircled with large trees, with campsites, a pool, and lovely flower gardens.

Huguette's restaurant rises in terraces, dominating the landscape. The setting is engaging, the menu more so.

These charming Meliets are pure Gascons. Fleeing the problems of working a family farm, she, a bookkeeper, and he, a former law student, decided on running a restaurant as a refuge "for the time being." She liked to cook and did it well.

"Our only baggage was family preserves and preserving vats. I made local dishes for our guests, the same ones I made for us, the same ones I have always made. Progress, yes, I've made some. Let us say that I have perfected dishes with constant care to stay within the authenticity of this region of mine.

"This is very desirable poultry-raising country because here that has remained an art. Corn fattens our geese, our ducks, and so on.

"Winter is goose season. Geese lay only once a year and they brood in the spring. Not so ducks. They are abundant layers and can hatch all year round, and the broods develop quickly. Adult ducks take to fattening. Thus the vogue for fresh duck liver and for duck fillets has grown—it's because they are always in season.

"The duck fillets I cook over coals, grilled over the embers of either grape vine shoots or peach trees. I do the livers with grapes, *au naturel*, the hearts and gizzards in a ragout with beans or even on a skewer with slices of duck breast. You can do anything. You can use all of a duck, just as you can a goose.

"In season I keep the goose carcasses after the flesh has been used. Grilled over a fire of grape vine shoots they can be picked clean and crunched with gourmandise.

"Yes, we live in a privileged region. Our spring vegetables are the prime ones for sale in Paris and our strawberries aren't just anonymous berries, they are *frais du Gers*."

This young woman, a blue-eyed brunette, tall and slim, everything about her elegant, loses her shyness when she talks about cooking. One understands how in four years she has made Le Moulin de Poüy a known gastronomic stopover.

SOUPE AUX FÈVES
Broad bean soup

ℐℐℐ

SERVES 6

This is more than a soup. Added to it is a very typical Languedoc stuffing of preserved duck gizzard, and in addition to the familiar soup herbs, there is the wild fragrance of hyssop.

2¼ pounds shelled young broad beans (about 6½–7 pounds with shells) (see note)
4 medium onions
2 cloves garlic
goose or chicken fat
6 duck gizzards
6 preserved duck wings

2 duck backs, cut into 6 pieces
1 bouquet garni of celery stalks or celery leaves and parsley stems
1 small bouquet garni of chives and hyssop (about 1 tablespoon dried), tied up in cheesecloth

Stuffing

2 preserved duck gizzards
2–3 chicken livers
10 ounces fresh, unsmoked bacon
4 shallots
1 tablespoon chopped parsley

1 cup bread crumbs made from the white part of the bread, dried and crumbled
3 whole eggs
salt and pepper
1 teaspoon sugar

Bring 13 cups salted water to a boil, add the beans, and lower the heat. Chop the onions and garlic and cook them until they are soft, but not brown, in a skillet with goose or chicken fat. Put the contents of the skillet into the bean water, add the 6 gizzards, wings, and pieces of back, then add the herb bouquets. Cook all together at a low boil for 45 minutes (with fresh beans; for dried beans see note).

Stuffing

Peel the skins off the gizzards and chop them finely with the livers, bacon, shallots, and parsley. Mix in the bread crumbs, eggs, salt, pepper, and sugar. Melt some more goose or chicken fat in a large frying pan, and then cook the stuffing as you would an omelette. When the bottom is firm fold it into thirds like a business letter. Then turn the folded stuffing over in the pan so the opening is down and seal it with the heat.

Bring the soup back to a simmer, and the moment it begins to simmer, slide in the stuffing, being careful not to break it. Let it cook without boiling for 30 minutes.

Remove the bouquets.

To serve, distribute a good slice of the stuffing, a giblet, a piece of back, and a wing into each bowl and cover with beans and soup. Serve with thick slices of toasted French bread.

NOTES: In the winter you may replace the fresh beans with dried white beans such as California small white beans, but then the soup has to cook for about 1½ hours or the beans have to be soaked overnight before cooking.

A number of the ingredients in the recipe are difficult to find in this country, but you can make substitutions. For the preserved wings and gizzards you can use fresh wings and fresh gizzards. But if you do use fresh gizzards, add a small can of inexpensive duck liver pâté to the stuffing for the taste. If you can't find goose fat, substitute chicken fat. Don't use duck fat because the fat from American ducks is not tasty.

Hyssop is hard to find but is available, dried, at old-fashioned drugstores or extremely comprehensive pharmacies.

If you can't find fresh bacon use fresh ham.

PÂTÉ PUR PORC
Pure pork pâté

✑ ✑ ✑

FOR AN 8-CUP TERRINE OR 2 BREAD PANS 9 BY 5 BY 3 INCHES

4½ pounds pork neck, boned
  and finely chopped
5–6 ounces pork liver
3 shallots
4 teaspoons salt

freshly ground pepper
1 piece caul fat to line the
  bottom and sides of the
  terrine
2 bay leaves

Preheat the oven to 350°F.

Chop the meats and shallots very finely, then mix carefully with salt and pepper. Don't taste to see if you have seasoned it enough (this is raw pork), but you can fry a little bit in a pan and taste that to judge.

Rinse the caul fat in warm, very salted water, then use it to line the terrine. Fill the lined dish with the pork mixture, then cross the overlap at the sides over the top of the pâté to cover. Cut off excess. Place the bay leaves on the surface. Cover with the top of the terrine or, if you don't have one, with a piece of aluminum foil. Place in the oven.

It shouldn't bubble over, but it should cook for about 1½ hours and, if necessary, you can check and lower the heat. Let cool in the turned-off oven with the door open.

When it is cool, put a piece of wood or something the size of the top of the terrine on it to tamp it down and compact the pâté without squashing it. When it has cooled completely keep it in the refrigerator.

NOTE: To weight down the pâté as it cools, use several pieces of heavy cardboard, then cover them with a book.

FOIE DE CANARD AUX RAISINS
Duck liver with grapes

℘℘℘

SERVES 5 TO 6

1 generous cup fresh grapes,
    any kind
21–24 ounces fresh duck liver
salt and pepper
½ cup Armagnac

Before beginning the cooking—which is very quick—peel and seed the grapes. Put the liver into an earthenware casserole or a small iron one. Add salt and pepper. Over very low heat cook the liver until it "sweats," that is until it becomes stiffened and heated through and gives off its fat. This should take about 20 minutes. Meanwhile, put the grapes into a small saucepan and heat gently.

Pour the rendered fat off the liver and cut the liver into slices about ½ inch thick. Dab both faces of each piece with Armagnac.

Return the liver to the casserole with the heated grapes and cook until everything is just reheated through. Serve on hot plates with slices of toast.

NOTES: It is very difficult to find so much duck liver in this country, and chicken liver can be substituted very well. It should still be cooked for 20 minutes, but it won't give off fat the same way duck liver will. It should stiffen though, and when it is done there will be liquid to pour off. Also, it need not be sliced, as it is already in small enough pieces, so just dab the Armagnac on whole chicken livers.

Peeling grapes is very difficult and tiresome and unless you are really a perfectionist this dish does not suffer from having them unpeeled. They do, however, have to be seeded, unless you use seedless grapes.

MAIGRETS AUX PÊCHES
Duck breasts with peaches

✑✑✑

8 breast fillets from large ducks
  (1 whole breast per person)
chicken fat or vegetable oil
8 unpeeled garlic cloves

salt and pepper
4 medium-size ripe peaches or
  canned without sugar
⅓ cup cider vinegar

Prepare the fillets by removing the skin. They will be like minute steaks.

Lightly grease a large skillet or sauté pan with chicken fat or oil and arrange the breasts in it. Heat until they stiffen and brown slightly, then turn them over. As you do add the unpeeled garlic and salt and pepper and cover the pan. This cut of meat is very much like a small steak, so treat it the way you would an individual steak. Cook it rare, medium, etc., to your taste. Gourmets like it so that it is bloody when you cut into it, but cooked through.

While the fillets are cooking, peel and quarter the peaches. When the meat is done to your taste, remove it from the pan and keep it hot but don't prolong the cooking. Remove the garlic cloves from the pan and pour off excess oil.

Put the peeled, quartered peaches into the pan and turn up the heat to brown them slightly. Pour in the vinegar in a thin stream and stir and scrape to deglaze. Bring to a boil, then immediately pour over the fillets. Serve very hot on hot plates.

SALMIS DE PALOMBES
Salmi of wood pigeon

⚹⚹⚹

SERVES 6

3 wood pigeons
goose or chicken fat
¾ cup Armagnac, warmed
2 onions, minced
2 shallots, minced
1 clove garlic, crushed

10 ounces unsmoked bacon,
  chopped fine
1 bottle good Bordeaux,
  warmed
salt and pepper
6 slices good white bread

Cut the pigeons in half along the breastbones and the spines. Remove the hearts, livers, gizzards, and backbones and set them aside. Remove the rest of the bones, leaving the wings and legs attached to their bones. These are the "meats."

Melt a tablespoon of goose or chicken fat in a large, heavy casserole and cook the backs, bones, and meats over low heat.

When the flesh has stiffened, sprinkle with the warm Armagnac and flame. Stand back—this is a lot of alcohol. Remove the meats and set them aside wrapped in foil.

To what remains in the casserole add the minced onions and shallots, the crushed garlic, and the chopped bacon. Cook, stirring, without letting it brown. In a large saucepan flame the wine, moving the saucepan gently so it burns well. Pour the flamed wine into the casserole and add salt and pepper. Cover the top of the casserole with a piece of waxed paper to seal it, then put on the cover. This will keep the stock from evaporating away as it simmers over very low heat for 2 hours.

During this time cook the livers, hearts, and gizzards in a little of the fat of your choice, then grind in a blender, food processor, or food mill to make a smooth purée.

When the stock has cooked, strain, pressing on the solids in the strainer to get out all the juices. Reduce the strained stock over high heat if necessary: there shouldn't be very much. Whisk several spoonfuls of boiling stock into the innards paste, then return it to the pot to thicken the sauce.

Return the meats to the stock along with any juices they might have given off in the foil while waiting. Cook them, without boiling, for 8–10 minutes. Correct the seasoning. While the last cooking is going on, fry the bread slices in the fat of your choice, and arrange them on a heated serving platter. Put a bird on each piece of bread and spoon the sauce over them.

This method of preparation is good for any wild fowl: doves, woodcock, wild duck, etc.

COQUELETS CRAPAUDINE AU BARBECUE
Barbecued split fryers

ℐℐℐ

SERVES 6

3 small frying chickens
goose fat, melted
2 hard-boiled eggs, finely
   chopped
2 shallots, minced

cider vinegar
olive oil
chervil
salt and pepper

Split the chickens down their backs, but leave them attached at the breast. Cut off the wing tips and take out the hearts, livers, and gizzards, then flatten the birds. Heat the barbecue until you have nicely glowing coals, no flames or smoke, then put the birds onto the grill, cut side down.

As the birds are cooking, paint them with the melted goose fat. Use a feather as Huguette Meliet does, or use a supple brush.

When the undersides are hot, turn the birds over on the grill and brown the fleshy parts.

Meanwhile, make a vinaigrette by combining the rest of the ingredients.

Remove birds from the fire and sprinkle with salt and pepper to taste.

Serve with the chervil vinaigrette.

NOTES: If you don't have goose fat you can baste with a little melted butter.

The vinaigrette will be a good temperature for the hot birds if you hard-boil the eggs as the birds are cooking, then put all the ingredients into a blender and blend together just before serving.

PASTIS DU GERS
Gers pastry

༄ ༄ ༄

This is a tart made with pâte feuilletée and filled with apples, plums, or apricots according to the season.

1 pinch salt	4–5 apples, not too juicy
1 tablespoon granulated sugar	⅔ cup extra-fine sugar
3 tablespoons vegetable oil	2 tablespoons vanilla sugar
3 cups flour	2 tablespoons Armagnac
18 ounces (4½ sticks) butter	

The day before you want to serve this dessert make the pastry. Put 1 cup of cold water, the salt, the granulated sugar, and the oil into a bowl. Add the flour little by little, mixing with your fingers. This is called the *détrempe*.

When all the ingredients are incorporated, the dough should be supple but not soft. Form into a ball—it should hold its shape.

Wrap in aluminum foil, then slip into a plastic bag and let rest in the refrigerator overnight (or for at least 3 hours). This amount of dough is enough for two 9-inch tarts. Cut the dough in half and leave the part you aren't working with in the refrigerator.

Preheat the oven to 450°F.

All of the rolling is made much easier if you use a pastry cloth and lots of flour.

Use a rolling pin and roll the dough out into a rectangle

three times as long as wide. Scatter half the butter, in little pieces, over the dough, leaving a 1-inch margin all around. Wet the border slightly and fold the dough in thirds as you would a business letter. Press with the flat of your hand, then roll out again into the same rectangle shape. Handle carefully at this stage so you don't tear the dough and let the butter escape. Fold in thirds again, turn your dough 180 degrees, roll out, and fold into thirds again. You have now made two turns. Do the complete process once more.

As the layers of dough get thinner, you will have to keep using lots of flour on your pastry board so the butter doesn't leak out and stick. If the dough should break though, just fold the broken part to the inside on the next turn.

As you work with it the pastry will become supple. On the last turn, form it into a rectangle the width of the baking sheet you will be using and twice as long.

Butter the sheet and sprinkle it with a little extra-fine sugar, then shake off the excess. Spread the pastry out on the buttered and sugared surface. Leave the excess, and don't trim any overlap.

Slice the apples very thin and arrange the slices over the pastry, leaving a 1-inch margin all the way around. Mix together the rest of the extra-fine sugar with 1 tablespoon of the vanilla sugar and sprinkle it over the apples generously but not excessively. Sprinkle lightly with Armagnac; the apples should not be too wet or the seal in the pastry won't hold. Paint the border of the dough with Armagnac, then fold the excess half over the apple-covered half to enclose it. Using a rolling pin seal the edges and now get rid of any overlapping dough.

Repeat with the reserved half of the dough and the remaining butter.

Put into the 450°F. oven for 15 minutes, then, without opening the oven door, turn the heat down to 400°F. Cook for another 7 minutes, then check the color and the bottom, which should get crisp. When the top has risen and the pastry is rigid, it is ready.

Sprinkle with the remaining tablespoon of vanilla sugar as soon as you remove from the oven. Serve warm.

NOTE: The apples in this tart shouldn't be too juicy or when they cook they will give off their liquid and leak out of the pastry shell.

This is a leaky tart to bake anyway, and to save your oven it will help to cook it over another, larger baking sheet, or better yet a jelly-roll pan which will hold the juices.

CÉLINE
MENNEVEAU

La Rôtisserie
du Chambertin
Gevrey-Chambertin (Côte d'Or)

Because her husband inherited a large farm, quite dilapidated but with wine cellars—actual church crypts from Roman times—Céline Menneveau became a chef. That's quickly said, but Madame Menneveau had already studied law and had a career as an auctioneer.

Naturally elegant, with admirable hands, she is a living

demonstration that intelligence and culture are powerful elements for succeeding in the minor arts from which cooking emerges. I contend that Céline Menneveau's cuisine is the art of an innately creative person.

She modestly says that she wanted to travel around France to acquire techniques she lacked. Thus she solicited the Troisgros brothers to accept her, at the bottom, humbly, to watch them going about their work. They did better. She followed them in all their operations. Ten days in their wake was enough for these masters to judge her. Her husband declares: "They returned her to me saying, 'She can fly all by herself.'"

We glance into her kitchen, where she works alone until the moment for service. We notice a basin filled with plump goose livers, which she is going to prepare in the afternoon. Rest is counted in minutes in this business; when one meal is finished one must begin to address oneself to the multiple details from toast to side dishes for the next. Everything must be planned ahead so it can be served rapidly, with serenity, as though you were the only guest.

The products are the same everyone uses, but stripped of affectations that violate their natural taste. That is one of the refinements of the renovated gastronomy—rejuvenated, rather.

Céline's menu is rich in entrées in which greens enrich slices of foie gras, such as calves' liver served hot on a bed of lamb's lettuce in season. What is really different is her use of various dressings: nut oils, olive oil, vinegars from the same sources as the notable wines.

Her oysters in champagne are incomparable, but when their season is over one forgets them for new productions of perennials such as her trout soufflé Céline. It is done like a mousse in a shrimp sauce, a knowledgeably arranged bouquet of flavors to eat before a whole pigeon à l'ancienne—the recipe for which she has confided.

Monsieur Menneveau presides over the dining room service. He is a combination captain, maître d', and sommelier. His wine cellar is his pride. He built it up himself and has become very familiar with the local harvests.

HUÎTRES CHAUDES AU CHAMPAGNE
Hot oysters in champagne sauce

ℐ ℐ ℐ

SERVES 4

16 large oysters	4 shallots
1 split (6.3 ounces) dry	½ teaspoon lemon juice
domestic champagne	2 egg yolks
4 ounces (1 stick) butter	salt and pepper

Open the oysters and empty the shells over a bowl to catch all the liquor. Save one shell from each oyster, wash it, and set it aside to keep warm in a low oven.

Strain the oyster liquor through cheesecloth, then put it and about ½ cup of the champagne into a small saucepan. Add the oysters and heat gently. When the oysters are warm, remove them with a slotted spoon and set aside, covered.

In the top of a double boiler, over direct heat, melt 3 tablespoons of the butter. Mince the shallots, put them into the butter, and cook, without letting them brown, until they are soft and transparent. When they are ready, add the liquid in which you poached the oysters, then the rest of the champagne. Over high heat reduce to a scant 2 tablespoons. This will take some time. Keep a careful eye on it toward the end—it will be very syrupy and could easily burn at this stage. If necessary, lower the heat. Add the lemon juice.

Bring water to a simmer in the bottom of the double boiler, then place the top, with its contents, over it. Keeping the sauce warm in this way, beat in the yolks with a wire whisk, then, bit by bit, stir in the rest (5 tablespoons) of the butter until the sauce is the consistency of a mayonnaise. Remove the top of the double boiler from the heat and correct seasoning.

Put the warm shells on an ovenproof dish, place an oyster in each, and spoon the sauce on to cover each oyster.

Run under the broiler for a minute to reheat a little and tan the sauce slightly. It is important that the sauce not get too hot or it will turn.

Note : Opening an oyster isn't easy, and the simplest way is to ask your fish man to sell you the oysters on the half shell. But then, because you won't have the liquor, you should substitute about ½ cup clam juice in the sauce.

TERRINE DE LAPEREAU EN GELÉE
Pâté of young rabbit in aspic

1 young rabbit, 2½ pounds
thin slices of fatback or
   blanched bacon to line the
   terrine
1 pound carrots, minced
1 pound onions, minced

¾ tablespoon juniper berries,
   coarsely crushed
salt and pepper
1 bay leaf
1 sprig thyme
½ cup plum liqueur

Completely bone the rabbit and cut the meat into thin strips. Save the bones. Line the inside of a terrine or bread pan with the strips of fat.

Preheat oven to 350°F.

Mix the onions with the carrots and put a third of the mixture into the bottom of the terrine in as smooth a layer as possible. Cover with a layer of half the rabbit strips. Salt and pepper and sprinkle with half the crushed juniper berries. Continue in this order, seasoning both layers of rabbit, and ending with the last vegetable layer. Top with a bay leaf and a sprig of thyme and moisten with the plum liqueur.

Cover the terrine with a piece of aluminum foil and place in a large, shallow ovenproof pan; then pour hot, but not boiling, water into the larger dish to come halfway up the sides of the terrine. Bake for 5 hours at 350°F., but check from time to time, and lower the temperature if the water starts to boil.

Gelée

the rabbit bones
1 calf's foot, split lengthwise
1 bouquet garni (parsley, bay
   leaf, thyme)
salt and pepper

While the terrine is cooking, boil the bones and head (if you have it) of the rabbit with the split calf's foot and the bouquet garni in 8 cups water. After 4 hours strain and degrease the gelée by pouring it through a moistened, folded-in-two tea towel. Reduce the strained liquid to 2 cups, season it carefully, and pour it into the terrine as it comes out of the oven. Let cool, then chill.

NOTE: If you don't want to make your own gelée from scratch you can bring 2 cups good beef consommé to a boil and stir in 1 envelope unflavored gelatin dissolved in a little cold water just before pouring into the terrine.

OEUFS EN MEURETTE
Poached eggs on toast with a red wine sauce

SISISI

SERVES 6

½ pound blanched bacon
2–3 cloves garlic
½ pound small mushrooms
1 teaspoon lemon juice
3 ounces (¾ stick) butter
12 small white onions
1 pinch sugar

1 tablespoon flour
salt and pepper
1 cup white wine vinegar
12 eggs, as fresh as you can find
12 slices good white bread,
   toasted

Sauce bourguignonne

1 chicken carcass and
   trimmings
1 bottle red burgundy
1 onion

1 bouquet garni (thyme,
   parsley, bay leaf)
1 carrot
5 peppercorns

Sauce

Chop the chicken carcass into smallish pieces, and place it in a large saucepan with all the other ingredients for the sauce. Cook for 40 minutes.

Strain through a dampened tea towel to degrease. Rinse out the pot, then return the stock to it, and reduce to about 2½ cups.

Cut the bacon into small pieces, dry it, and brown it in a frying pan with the garlic. Remove the bacon and garlic with a slotted spoon and discard the fat. Set the solids aside in a little stock, scooped from the reducing pot.

Cut the mushrooms into halves or quarters (they should be about the same size as the pieces of bacon) and put them into a large saucepan with just enough water to come half-way up their sides. Add the lemon juice and 3 tablespoons of the butter. Bring to a boil over high heat and cook until the water has evaporated and only butter is left.

Add the set-aside bacon and garlic to the mushrooms in the buttery saucepan. Then add the onions, enough water to cover, and a pinch of sugar. Boil until again there is no more water, then add the entire contents of the saucepan to the sauce they have been resting in.

Heat the sauce. Cream the remaining 3 tablespoons butter with the flour, then bit by bit stir it into the sauce, off the heat.

Stir to mix, bring to a boil, stirring constantly, then turn off the heat and let stand, covered. Taste and correct seasoning.

Poaching

In a large flat pan, such as a *sautoir* or an old-fashioned skillet, heat 2½ inches of water. Add the vinegar. Just before the water comes to a boil—don't let it—break a very fresh egg into a teacup. Put the cup flush with the water line, tilt it, and slide the egg into the water.

It will sink to the bottom but will rise, by itself, when some of the white coagulates. Help it carefully with a wooden spoon. Turn it over and spoon some of the white over the top so it doesn't float around but makes a compact bundle. Let it cook for about 3½ minutes. It should be firm, and you will be able to remove it with a slotted spoon onto a kitchen towel. You should be able to poach four or five eggs at once. While they are cooking bring the sauce back to a boil. Also bring the sauce with the garlic, bacon, mushrooms, and onions to a boil.

Arrange each egg on its toast and spoon boiling sauce over each one. Then sprinkle the onions, mushrooms, and bacon over them. Serve very hot.

COQUILLES SAINT-JACQUES AU SAFRAN
Scallops with saffron sauce

♗ ♗ ♗

La nage is a delicately flavored court bouillon for poaching shellfish—elegant crustaceans such as scallops and lobsters. It is easy and quick to cook, and if you don't use it as the basis for your sauce as you do in this recipe, it is good to use the same *nage* over and over several times—the flavor improves. So save it in a glass jar in your refrigerator. It is also wonderful as the basis for very refined sauces.

Nage

4 carrots
8–10 small onions or large
  scallions
1 clove garlic
the white of 1 medium leek
3 stalks celery
1 bouquet garni (thyme, bay
  leaf, parsley)

1 sprig tarragon or 2 leaves
  sage (¼ teaspoon of either if
  dried)
salt and white pepper
coriander
1 clove
1 pinch cayenne
1 pinch saffron threads

Cut the carrots into rounds. Choose small onions or large firm scallions. Put the carrots and onions or scallions into a stock pot with the garlic, the white of the leek, well washed, and the celery stalks. Add the bouquet garni, tarragon or sage, salt, and about 5 turns of a pepper mill of white pepper. Add about the same amount of coriander, the clove, a tiny pinch of cayenne, and an equally tiny pinch of saffron threads. (Be sure to use the threads—saffron is not always so pure if it is powdered.) Add 2 quarts of water.

Cook over high heat, covered, at a vigorous boil, for 7–10 minutes. The vegetables should still be crisp. Let the *nage* stand, as is, vegetables in the liquid, until it is cool.

Scallops
3 pounds scallops

If scallops are large, halve or even quarter them. They should be about the size of hazelnuts.

Place the scallops in a wide casserole, large enough so that they will fit in one layer. Heat the *nage* just to the boiling point, then pour it—through a strainer—over the scallops to cover them. Cook, taking care to maintain the liquid just at the simmer, for 4 minutes.

Drain off and save the cooking liquid. Cover the casserole and keep the scallops warm, but don't let them continue to cook.

The sauce

the reduced *nage*
about 1 cup vermouth
about 1 cup heavy cream
saffron

lemon
chervil and chives (1 table-
spoon fresh, ½ teaspoon if
dried)

Boil the *nage* until it is reduced to about 1 cup. Measure it, then add equal amounts of vermouth and cream. Also add several threads of saffron soaked in an egg cup of the boiling *nage*, and several drops of lemon juice. Return the sauce to a boil and drop in a generous tablespoon of chervil cut up with scissors and an equal amount of chives. Pour over the scallops in the casserole and let stand for 5 minutes. Serve hot but not boiling.

NOTE : Saffron should be used only as a very light coloring in this recipe. Its flavor, which is very concentrated, is delicious, but only in tiny doses.

PIGEONS À L'ANCIENNE
Roast pigeon with cream sauce

SSS

SERVES 6

6 small pigeons, or 3 larger
   ones
4½ ounces (1 stick plus 1
   tablespoon) butter, softened

12 cloves garlic, unpeeled
salt and pepper
1 cup good dry white wine
1 cup heavy cream

Preheat oven to 450°F.

Set aside the pigeons' livers, then butter each bird well, using 8 tablespoons (1 stick) of the butter. Put two cloves of *unpeeled* garlic and salt and pepper in the cavity of each bird (four garlic cloves in each cavity if pigeons are large), then place them on a rack in a roasting pan and roast, basting frequently. When the birds are puffed and golden, prick them with a skewer or the point of a knife; the juices should run golden if the birds are done. When they are, remove them from the oven and keep them warm, but don't let them cook any longer or they will dry out.

While the pigeons are roasting, cook their livers in the remaining tablespoon of butter. After the birds are done, take the garlic out of their cavities, peel the cloves, and mash them—in a blender or a mortar and pestle—with the livers to make a paste.

Take the pigeons out of the roasting pan and set aside on a heated platter. Remove the fat from the pan and deglaze with the wine. Bring to a boil, scraping up the cooked-on bits with a wooden spoon. Add the cream and reduce over high heat until the sauce coats a spoon.

Add the liver paste, taste, and correct the seasoning.

Serve the pigeons with their sauce spooned over them.

If the pigeons are large, serve them cut in half, half to each person.

NOTE: You can easily substitute in this recipe. If you want to use squab (which are pigeons) serve one to a person, or if you prefer Rock Cornish game hens, serve half.

GÂTEAU AU CHOCOLAT AMER
Bittersweet chocolate cake

ℐℐℐ

FOR A 10-BY-3-INCH CAKE PAN OR SPRINGFORM

This cake keeps for a long time in the refrigerator, so don't hesitate to prepare it ahead of time for important occasions.

> 14 ounces bittersweet chocolate
> (the darkest you can find)
> 12 eggs, separated
> 2 cups sugar
> 14 ounces (3½ sticks) butter,
> soft but not melted
> 1 cup flour, measured then sifted

Grate the chocolate or break it into small pieces. Place in the top of a double boiler with 3 tablespoons of cold water. Keep the water in the bottom of the double boiler simmering, and melt the chocolate without taking it off the simmering water or it will crystallize. It will take 30 minutes to carry out this essential step. Let the chocolate cool somewhat.

Preheat oven to 325°F. and adjust rack to the middle level of your oven.

Butter and sugar the cake pan and knock out any excess sugar.

Beat the yolks with the 2 cups of sugar just until they form a ribbon when they fall from the beaters. Add the tepid chocolate, then the very soft butter and the sifted flour. Mix thoroughly. Beat the egg whites until very stiff, then stir a spoonful into the chocolate mixture to lighten it. Fold the rest of the whites into the chocolate mixture, being very careful when lifting the heavier chocolate mixture up from the bottom and folding it over. If you aren't careful at this stage and lose the air you have beaten into the whites, when you take your cake out of the oven it will fall and will be heavy.

Turn the batter into the prepared pan. There should be about an inch of room at the top. The cake shouldn't rise, but it will inflate a little and fill that space. Place in the preheated oven. During the baking the outside of the cake will form a crust enclosing an interior which should be creamy but not liquid. Test with your finger to see if the cake is done: a firm exterior and a squashy center. This will take about 1 hour and 20 minutes. Then turn off heat and let the cake cool in the oven. Then refrigerate. Serve cold.

NOTES: Several tablespoons of Grand Marnier or Curaçao added with the egg whites are very good.

The top of the cake will sink as it cools. To make it look prettier, cover the top with sifted confectioners' sugar.

DOMINIQUE
NAHMIAS

Olympe
Paris 14ᵉ

Dominique Olympe Nahmias, age twenty-six, is, she says, the youngest woman chef running a restaurant in France.

She was twenty-two when she "arrived" in Paris with her sociologist husband and their very young son to open a pastry shop in a little store on the rue Montparnasse.

She had spent five years studying acting at the Toulon conservatory. However, in less than one year she created a style, a talent which fills her small dining room every night from eight until twelve, if not later.

A dozen tables in a vaguely old-fashioned setting, made silent by the crimson velvet portières. There are banquettes with numerous cushions and several chairs, and there is scarcely room to push your chair back and look over the whole thing.

All alone in her minuscule kitchen she makes everything herself. Organization and method are imperative with her. Her sense of measure, her inventive genius, and her well-tempered daring make her the incarnation of the *nouvelle cuisine*: rigorously chosen produce, light sauces, and carefully watched cooking.

Salmon, raw or in a stew with truffles; transparently thin slices of raw fillet; San Daniele ham from Venice; fresh pâté, made in the house; vegetable terrine; lamb with small preserved onions—extracts from her menu.

These are listed above her wonderful dessert: little porcelain cups loaded with cold mousse: white, chartreuse, beige (with nuts and with nougat), pink (raspberry sherbet). A fresh fruit cup: pear, pineapple, grapes—a fresh raspberry sauce. A slice of lemon tart, another of chocolate cake.

And then the post of irresistible tisanes come: linden-mint, verbena-mint, assorted. The lovely flowered plates— I almost forgot to mention them, so concerned was I with gathering recipes from the astonishing Olympe.

TARTE À LA TOMATE ET AU BASILIC
Tomato and zucchini tart

ʃʃʃ

Pastry

1⅔ cups flour

5 ounces (1¼ sticks) butter,
  softened

1 egg

salt

1 tablespoon butter for the plate

Place the flour in a pile on the table or counter. Add the butter, very softened but not melted, the whole egg, and a pinch of salt. Using your fingers mix in the flour so that it becomes absorbed little by little.

As soon as the dough is amalgamated, form it into a ball, wrap it in waxed paper, and set aside in the refrigerator for at least 30 minutes.

Butter a 10-inch pie plate or quiche dish. Preheat oven to 400°F.

Sprinkle the work surface lightly with flour. Flatten the dough with your hand, then roll it out into a rectangle. Fold it in three, as you would a business letter, then repeat the process. And again. After the third turn the dough should be smooth and supple. Roll out once more, about ¼ inch thick, and place in the buttered plate.

Cover the dough with a piece of aluminum foil, then pour dried beans or rice in to fill. This will weigh the bottom down so the crust doesn't rise, and the foil will keep the rice or beans out of the crust. Prick the pastry several times with the point of a knife through the foil and bake for 35–40 minutes. Check to be sure the bottom is cooked through.

Filling

2 pounds tomatoes
salt and pepper
olive oil
4 medium zucchini
1 tablespoon chopped fresh basil

While the crust is cooking prepare the filling.

Peel the tomatoes and slice them in half around the equator. Cut off the stem scar, remove the seeds with a grapefruit knife or other small knife, and salt and pepper the cavities. Heat a little olive oil in a frying pan over low heat and half-cook the tomatoes, cut sides down. They should still be fairly crunchy; don't let them get too soft. Remove and drain.

Slice the unpeeled zucchini into thin rounds and brown them in the olive oil. Add salt and pepper.

If you are not going to fill the hot crust immediately, set both vegetables aside in the refrigerator. When you are ready to cook the tart begin filling the crust, zucchini on the bottom, then a sprinkle of chopped basil, then the tomatoes and more basil.

Cook another 15 minutes in a 400°F. oven and serve warm.

SALADE D'ÉCREVISSES AUX ARTICHAUTS
Crayfish salad with artichokes

ℐ ℐ ℐ

SERVES 6

24 crayfish	a good vinegar
6 artichokes	salt and pepper
juice of 1 lemon	olive oil
2 tablespoons flour	2 tablespoons chopped parsley

Bring 8 cups well-salted water to a boil. While it is coming to the boil, clean the crayfish, removing the black intestine down the back and the sac it's attached to. Wash the crayfish quickly, then toss them into the boiling water. When the water returns to the boil cook for 5 minutes, then remove the crayfish from the water and refresh them under cold running water.

Don't cut the stems off the artichokes—break them off. They should carry away with them the stringy parts of the bottom, which are unpleasant to chew.

Using a very sharp kitchen knife, cut the leaves off flush with the bottom. Then, the way you would peel a potato, cut off any remaining hard leaves. Leave the choke—you can get rid of that when the artichokes are cooked. Roll the bottoms around in lemon juice to keep them from darkening.

Drop the flour into 8 cups cold, salted water, stir to dissolve the flour, then bring to a boil. Add the artichokes and cook until they are *al dente*, that is to say, still firm to the teeth. When they can be pierced with the point of a knife—but not too easily—they are ready. Refresh them under cold running water. When they are lukewarm remove the chokes and cut each bottom into 6–8 pieces. Let them marinate at room temperature in a vinaigrette of fine vinegar, salt, pepper, olive oil, and the parsley, until ready to serve.

Remove and reserve the crayfish heads and claws. Peel the bodies.

This delicate salad should be served on small individual plates with the pieces of artichoke and the crayfish mixed and each serving decorated with 4 crayfish heads and claws around the edges of the plate.

NOTE: Shrimp may be substituted for the crayfish. You will need 1½ pounds.

DARNES DE SAUMON EN PAPILLOTES
Salmon steaks in wrappers

SS SS SS

SERVES 6

10 ounces fresh sorrel (you will
  want about ¾ cup, cut up, for
  each steak)
6 salmon steaks, about 2–3
  inches thick
salt and pepper
6 ounces (1½ sticks) butter

Preheat oven to 400°F.

Tear off pieces of aluminum foil large enough to wrap
each slice of salmon hermetically.

Cut the sorrel into pieces with scissors and, using half of
it, make a bed of it on each piece of aluminum foil. Put a
slice of salmon on each sorrel bed. Sprinkle with salt and
pepper, then cover with the rest of the sorrel, and put 2
tablespoons of butter into each packet. Fold up the foil and
seal.

Put into the preheated oven, placing the packets directly
on the oven rack. Cook for 15–20 minutes depending on the
size of the steak. Turn off the oven and keep warm until
ready to serve. Open the packages on hot plates.

CIVET DE GIGOT AUX
OIGNONS FRAIS CONFITS
Sliced leg of lamb with fresh glazed onions

𝒮𝒮𝒮

SERVES 6

8 ounces (2 sticks) butter
2 tablespoons minced shallots
1½ bottles Cabernet or Brouilly
1 bouquet garni (parsley, thyme,
   bay leaf, rosemary)

1¼ pounds small white onions
salt and pepper
1 tablespoon extra-fine sugar
1 small leg of lamb
oil

Melt 4 tablespoons of the butter in a large saucepan and cook the minced shallots until they are soft. Don't let them brown. Add the wine and the bouquet garni and reduce, at a low boil, to two-thirds of the original amount. Strain and set aside in the saucepan.

In a deep frying pan place the whole, peeled onions and enough water to come one-third of the way up their sides. Dot with 4 tablespoons butter, and add salt, pepper, and the sugar.

Let cook uncovered at a low boil until the water has evaporated, leaving only the butter. Shake the pan from time to time. Lower the heat and glaze and brown the onions.

Using a large, sharp knife, slice the leg of lamb into six big slices, each one going the length of the leg. Rotate the leg as you slice—there is meat all the way around. Heat a little oil in a large frying pan and sauté the lamb slices. Leave them rare. Keep them warm, without prolonging the cooking, on a heated serving platter. Salt and pepper lightly.

Finish off the sauce. Bring back to a boil, add salt and pepper, and then, little by little, off the heat, stir in the remaining 8 tablespoons of butter, softened and cut in pieces. Arrange the very hot onions around the lamb on the serving platter, spoon a little sauce over everything, and serve on very hot plates with the rest of the sauce in a sauceboat.

TERRINE DE LÉGUMES
Vegetable pâté

 ⌒⌒⌒

SERVES 8 TO 10

1 head celery	2 apples
1 head fennel	fresh basil
4 small eggplants	salt and pepper
4 medium zucchini	1 pinch cumin
olive oil	fresh mint
4 tomatoes	

This is an unmolded terrine. It may be made either in large
molds (this amount will fill two 9-by-5-by-2-inch bread
pans) or in individual ovenproof molds, which is how it is
served at Olympe. It makes a lovely presentation.

All the vegetables in this dish should be sliced very thin;
try to keep them uniform.

String the celery. Cut it into pieces the length of your
molds. Do the same with the fennel. Blanch them together
in boiling salted water for 8–10 minutes.

Slice the unpeeled eggplants and zucchini lengthwise
into strips about ⅛ inch thick. Then cut to the size of your
mold. Fry them until lightly colored in olive oil, then drain
them on absorbent paper.

Preheat oven to 425°F.

Peel the tomatoes and the apples, and cut them into
thin vertical slices. Lightly oil your terrine, then begin filling
it with a bed of tomatoes, some basil, then a layer of apples,

then celery, then fennel. Salt and pepper moderately and sprinkle with cumin.

Now arrange a bed of eggplant, then zucchini, and top with the leaves from one or two sprigs of mint. Season with discretion as before and begin again arranging the vegetables in the same order, pressing down firmly after each series of layers. Continue until the terrine is full to within ½ inch of the top. Cover. If your mold doesn't have a lid, use a piece of aluminum foil. Bake for 20–25 minutes. To serve, unmold.

MANDARINES À L'ARMAGNAC
Mandarin oranges in Armagnac

ℐℐℐ

FOR TWO 1-QUART PRESERVING JARS

3½ pounds mandarin oranges
or small tangerines
2 cups extra-fine sugar
1 bottle young Armagnac

Peel the mandarins, which should be quite ripe, with firm, glossy skin. Keep them whole and get rid of all the white filament, without piercing the skin. This is possible to do if you can buy them without seeds, otherwise you have the choice of getting rid of the seeds at the same time that you're peeling them or warning guests they will have to spit. The peeling is a long, boring process, and somewhat painful to the fingernails. It is helpful if you can get assistance.

Put the oranges into preserving jars so that the jars are full but the oranges are not squashed. Pour in the sugar until it is three fingers high in the bottom of the jar. Knock the jars on the table to shake the sugar around between the fruits. Shake the fruit level again and slowly pour in Armagnac to fill.

Set the jars aside in a dark, cool place for 1 month. Turn the jars over once a week during that time so the sugar sifts to the bottom. If the sugar has dissolved entirely, add the same amount again and wait a full month before tasting the oranges.

You can use these to enliven a fruit salad, to flavor ice cream, custard, etc., or the way you would use any fruit preserved in alcohol.

JANINE
RAIBAUT-DUNAN

⚜⚜⚜

La Pignata d'Or
Grande-Corniche, Nice
(Alpes-Maritimes)

One has to scale Nice's *grande corniche* to read "La Pignata d'Or" on the façade of a modest house.

A *pignata*, in Niçoise dialect, is a stewpot. Janine's *pignata* is an ancient woodworking shop—one foot on the road, the other over the void—that's what one would say looking at it in profile. But it's solidly set among its hanging gardens. The gardens, where one can lounge, afford one an exceptional view of the Bay of Angels.

Janine Raibaut-Dunan is an authentic Niçoise. Alone in her kitchen, alone in serving nearly ten tables. "More, I can't manage, unless they order ahead. Every day I change my menu depending on what 'they' bring me." "They" are the market gardeners, the fishermen, the butchers in the neighborhood.

"I have no secrets. I cook the way my grandmother did. I still cook all my slow-cooking preparations over charcoal. You have to know cooking to master it. I use each spice carefully—none should dominate. It's the cooking process that makes everything—the texture of the sauce, you never boil it over high heat."

How did she start? Twenty years ago she left a tailor's backroom she had entered very young and where she had stayed for twenty years. "Air, air," she said, explaining her decision.

She directed the renovation of the old house with lots of imagination. She explains: the design of the floor, the olive trees supporting the roof beams, the shine on all the wood are all her work. It is her adroit hands which she moves so youthfully when she gestures to explain her pissaladière or her Niçoise stuffing.

"Oh, it isn't really a recipe, you know, you put in all the vegetables you have on hand: zucchini, eggplant, fresh onions, and cooked ham, eggs, Fribourg cheese. I like Fribourg better than any other cheese for gratins because it has a good taste. I put it on the table to sprinkle on my soupe au pistou."

SOUPE AU PISTOU
Provençal vegetable soup

☞☞☞

SERVES 6 TO 8

1 pound potatoes
½ pound (weighed in shell)
   broad beans, shelled, or
   6 ounces dried beans
4 ounces plump green beans
4 carrots

3 medium leeks
1 pound peas, weighed in pods
4 ounces blanched bacon
2–3 medium tomatoes, peeled,
   seeded, and coarsely chopped
4 zucchini

Dice the potatoes, and if you are using dried beans soak them until they have absorbed a lot of water and are inflated, then weigh them (they should weigh ½ pound). Cut the green beans into ½-inch pieces. Peel the carrots, then cut into a small dice. Slice the clean leeks into ½-inch rounds, and shell the peas.

Put them all in a kettle with 12 cups water and bring to a boil for 10 minutes, then add the bacon, cut into small pieces, the tomatoes, and the unpeeled zucchini cut into ½-inch rounds.

Keep cooking over very low heat (it should just simmer) for 2 hours, then stir the soup with a large fork to move it around and mix it without breaking up the vegetables any more than is necessary.

While it is cooking prepare the pistou.

Pistou
½ cup packed fresh basil leaves
2 cloves garlic
¼ cup grated Fribourg cheese
   (or Gruyère or Swiss)
olive oil

Crush the basil leaves with the garlic in a mortar and pestle. When they are a paste, add the grated cheese by spoonfuls and moisten with a little olive oil. When you are finished, you will have a smooth, but not liquid, paste. A blender is no good for this operation, but a food processor works well.

When you are ready to serve, drop the pistou into the boiling kettle and stir it in. Let boil for a moment, correct the seasoning, and serve immediately.

PÂTES FRAÎCHES ET LEUR SAUCE
Fresh pasta with sauce

✎ ✎ ✎

SERVES 6 TO 8

Pasta
3½ cups flour
2 eggs
salt

Sauce Dunan
7 ounces prosciutto   1 ounce dried mushrooms
2 tablespoons butter   thyme
2 tablespoons peanut oil   bay leaf
1 onion, chopped   salt and pepper
3 tomatoes

Cooking and serving
1 tablespoon peanut oil
Fribourg cheese, grated (see note)

Pasta
Pour the flour into a mound on a table or counter and make
a well in it. In the well, place the eggs, ½ cup of water,
and a large pinch of salt. Mix together with your fingers,
adding more water carefully as necessary to get a thick
dough, supple but not soft. Let rest 30 minutes while you get
the ingredients for the sauce ready (chop the prosciutto,
peel, seed, and chop the tomatoes, etc.).

When the dough has rested, break off little bits of it

Terrine de légumes

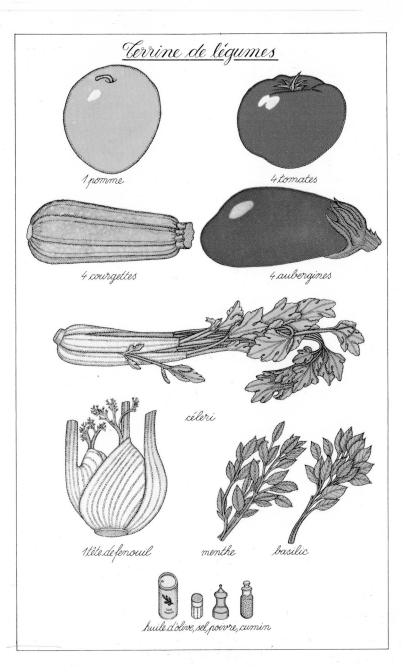

1 pomme

4 tomates

4 courgettes

4 aubergines

céleri

1 tête de fenouil

menthe

basilic

huile d'olive, sel, poivre, cumin

La soupe niçoise au pistou

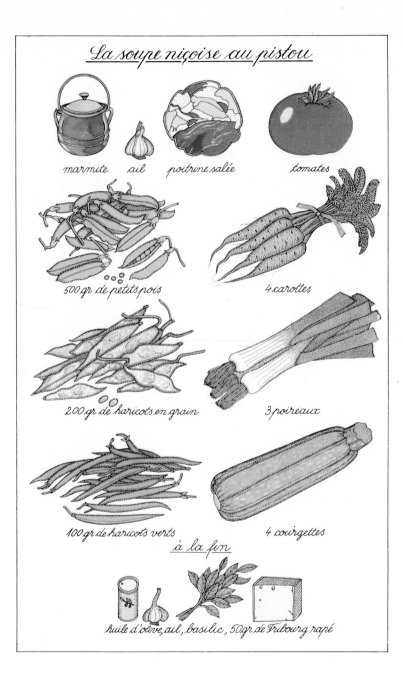

marmite   ail   poitrine salée   tomates

500 gr de petits pois   4 carottes

200 gr de haricots en grain   3 poireaux

100 gr de haricots verts   4 courgettes

à la fin

huile d'olive, ail, basilic, 50 gr de Fribourg rapé

and roll out with a pasta machine. Make the noodles thick at first, then bring the rollers closer and closer until the dough is supple as silk (about setting number 3 on the machine). Then, using the machine, cut dough into narrow or wide noodles, according to your taste, or into spaghetti.

Bring lots of boiling salted water to a boil and add 1 tablespoon peanut oil. Drop in the noodles and cook for 5 minutes. Serve well drained and buttered.

Sauce

Cut the prosciutto into little pieces. Heat 2 tablespoons butter and 2 tablespoons peanut oil in a large frying pan. When they are hot add the chopped prosciutto and chopped onion. Cook until the onion colors slightly.

Peel, seed, and chop the tomatoes, and plump the dried mushrooms in a small bowl of water. Add both to the frying pan, then add thyme and the bay leaf. Cook, stirring constantly, until the mixture turns into a paste; taste before adding salt and pepper—the prosciutto is salty.

Serve in a sauceboat accompanied by the grated Fribourg.

NOTES: Fribourg is very difficult to find, and a good Swiss or Gruyère is easier to get and a fine substitute. Just don't use Parmesan.

This pasta doesn't dry before cooking, so you are really doing the whole operation at once. If you like, you can make the pasta a few days ahead and cook it at the last minute, but if you want to do it all at once the most sensible order is:

1. Make the pasta dough.
2. While it is resting for the 30 minutes before rolling

out, peel the tomatoes, chop the prosciutto, put the mush-rooms in water to plump, chop the onion. Grate the cheese.

3. Roll out the pasta.

4. Bring the water to a boil and while you are waiting for it, make the sauce.

5. Let the sauce cook while the water boils. Drop the pasta into the water, return to the boil, cook 5 minutes at most, drain, and toss with butter.

6. Put the sauce in a sauceboat and serve with the pasta.

LAPIN AU PORTO
Rabbit in port

SERVES 6

1 young rabbit, about 3 pounds
2 tablespoons peanut oil
2 tablespoons butter
1 large onion, chopped
2 cloves garlic
3 branches thyme, or 1 teaspoon
   dried

1 bay leaf
1 tablespoon tomato paste
1 bottle red port
salt and pepper

Cut the rabbit into pieces. The easiest is two for the back, two for each hind leg, and four for the saddle and the front legs. Brown the pieces in the oil and butter over low heat. When they are well browned, add the chopped onion, garlic, thyme, bay leaf, and tomato paste. Stir to mix and heat well, then stir in the port to cover the pieces of rabbit. Add salt and pepper.

Let simmer uncovered for about 2 hours.

Serve with fresh pasta cooked *al dente*, which means firm but not crunchy.

DAUBE AUX CÈPES
Beef stew with mushrooms

𝒮𝒮𝒮

SERVES 6

¾ ounce dried cèpes
2½ pounds bottom round of
  beef
2 tablespoons peanut oil
1 large onion
2 cloves garlic

1 bay leaf
thyme
1 teaspoon tomato paste
salt and pepper
1 bottle red wine (a California
  burgundy is fine)

Let the cèpes soak for 6 hours in six times their volume of water (about 4 cups). Keep adding water as it is absorbed, so that there is always the same amount in the bowl.

Ask your butcher to cut the beef in stew-size pieces.

Brown the meat in a heavy casserole in the peanut oil. Halfway through add the onion, garlic, bay leaf, thyme, and tomato paste. Cover the pot and let stew for 30 minutes over medium heat.

Pour in the cèpes and their soaking water, add salt and pepper, and then pour in enough wine to come level with the top of the meat. Stir to mix, then let boil rapidly for several minutes.

Cover the pot and lower heat way down. Cook for 4–5 hours at a very gentle simmer. At the end of this time the meat should be tender and the sauce thick. Serve with macaroni or fresh buttered noodles.

GNOCCHI À L'ITALIENNE
Italian gnocchi

𝒢𝒢𝒢

SERVES 6

2–2¼ pounds boiling (not
   baking) potatoes
1¾ cups flour (approximately)
salt and pepper
butter
grated Gruyère or Swiss cheese,
   or Sauce Dunan (pp. 270–71)

Boil the potatoes in their skins. Peel them while they are still very hot and put them through a food mill or mash in a food processor. Add the flour, little by little, mixing and then kneading with your hands. Add salt and pepper and more flour until the dough stops sticking to the work surface and your hands.

Break off bits of dough and roll into cylinders about the size of a finger. Slice the cylinders into ½- to ¾-inch rounds, then one by one put a round of dough into the hollow of your palm and, using the back of the tines of a fork, press the dough into a cup shape. Keep flouring your hands and the back of the fork, or the dough will stick and you won't be able to do this step.

Bring 12 cups of lightly salted water to a boil and toss in the gnocchi a handful at a time. Don't cook too many at once or they will gum together at the bottom. When the dumplings rise to the surface they are cooked. Remove them with a slotted spoon and let drain on a towel while the others cook.

Serve with butter and grated cheese or with Sauce Dunan.

YVONNE · SOLIVA

Moulin de Tante Yvonne
Lambesc (Bouches-du-Rhône)

Madame Soliva, Tante Yvonne, has run three other restaurants and is still Tante Yvonne on Saturdays on radio Monte-Carlo.

A *moulin* (windmill) in the middle of town, in a village without a river nor sails to move in the wind! "Bloody mill," said she, ferreting out with her blue eyes the surprise in yours. A millstone for olives, a millstone for wheat, those fifteenth-century arches that draw "ahs" of admiration from you, a vast room, cool in summer, decorated with well-informed taste, inviting tables, welcome from the master of the house who treats you as an honored guest. And Tante Yvonne all in white, framed in the doorway of the kitchen. You know nothing banal awaits you here.

Who then is this Tante Yvonne?

Pure Marseilles blood, said she, passionate about cooking since her childhood to the point of purposely walking in puddles so she would be dried out by the stove—fascinated by its fires, its pots, its stocks.

Daughter of a jurist, wife of a lawyer, her first meals were for entertaining at home. A widow, she married young Soliva. They were the same age and he gave himself up to her passion: to create a restaurant where one could eat good cooking as served in a home, made by her in the good meridional tradition . . . but with her personal interpretations.

There are many refinements to her cooking. Her preserved truffles, that's easy. She envelops each truffle hermetically in aluminum foil, puts them in special boxes, and seals them in a pressure cooker, then freezes them. Thawed, submerged in water, what you wind up with is a truffle, flavored as it was on the first day.

Thyme: to dry it out well one must gather it wild, in flower, in May. The *fête du thyme* in Lambesc is May 2.

Garlic Pèbre is a provincial savory—it goes into everything but it shouldn't reveal itself. Only in a single sauce, but no other preparation, should its flavor dominate. Tante Yvonne never tastes as she cooks. Her fingers are precision scales for seasonings. She has created a gamut of aromas, which never varies. Even the saltiness is always the same.

Alone in her kitchen, everything is ready to use. It's

necessary to work fast, as nothing is cooked in advance. Intransigent about both the temperature of the food and of the plates, her microwave oven allows her—in several seconds —to reheat any dish to its original temperature without prolonging the cooking or turning the delicate liaisons.

This perfectionism has its drawbacks. She has to limit the number of her guests, unless they order ahead, and choose the same menu for everyone. Otherwise they would have to wait, and that she hates.

FLAN DE LANGOUSTE
AU BEURRE D'ÉCREVISSES
Lobster custard with shrimp butter

ℐℐℐ

Shrimp cooking liquid

3 tablespoons butter

1 carrot, grated

2 onions, minced

bouquet garni (thyme, bay
  leaf, parsley)

2 cups dry white wine

salt and pepper

Begin by preparing the shrimp cooking liquid, which will be the base for your sauce. Melt the butter in a large saucepan and gently stew the grated carrots, minced onions, and bouquet garni. When the onions are transparent but haven't taken on color, pour in the wine, add salt and pepper, and 2 cups of water. Let boil slowly for 30 minutes.

Sauce

12 jumbo shrimp

7 ounces (1¾ sticks) butter

1 tablespoon heavy cream, at
  room temperature

When the stock has cooked for 30 minutes, plunge in the shrimp. Five minutes after the liquid returns to the boil turn off the heat and let the shrimp cool in the stock. When they are cool, remove them with a slotted spoon and place the stock in the refrigerator.

Peel the shrimp. Save the shells and grind them in a mortar and pestle or a food processor. Weigh the resulting paste (it should be about 3 ounces) and add an equal weight of butter. Crush the shell paste and the butter together (again in the mortar or processor), then force through a sieve. What you end up with will be shrimp butter.

Add the buttery wastes left in the sieve to the stock. Heat and strain—now you may discard the wastes—then reduce to a scant 1 cup. Set aside in the refrigerator.

Lobster custard

2 cups milk	1 tablespoon pastis or anisette
1 lobster, 1½–2 pounds	4 eggs
salt and pepper	2 egg yolks
cayenne	1 tablespoon heavy cream

You will need six 8-ounce ovenproof dishes or seven 6-ounce ones (old-fashioned custard cups are good).

Scald the milk, then set aside in the refrigerator to chill. Kill the lobster by plunging it into boiling salted water. As soon as it stops wiggling take it out and drain it. Cut the tail off and return the front end to the boiling water for 15 minutes to finish cooking. Meanwhile peel the tail.

Divide the tail and as many scraps as you have among the six dishes. If there is any coral in the thorax remove and divide it, too. Take the meat out of the cooked claws and get any other edible meat. Cut it all up and divide it, too.

In a medium-size bowl mix a pinch of salt, a healthy grind of pepper, and a large pinch of cayenne with the pastis or anisette, the eggs and egg yolks whisked into the scalded, cold milk, and then the tablespoon of cream. Add a tablespoon of the butter risen to the top of the stock. (If you stored the stock in the refrigerator the butter will have risen and congealed and be very easy to retrieve.) Mix together and taste. Correct the seasoning; it should be spicy. Arrange the dishes on an ovenproof plate large enough to hold them and use as a bain marie. (A gratin dish is good for this.)

Preheat the oven to 350°F.

Pour the custard mixture into the dishes over the pieces of lobster, then pour hot water into the large dish to come halfway up the sides of the small ones. Cook in the preheated oven for 50 minutes to 1 hour. The custard is done when a knife stuck into one comes out clean and the mixture has pulled away from the sides a bit. Check occasionally to see that the water doesn't boil and, if it should, turn down your oven.

Heat the reduced cup of stock just to the boiling point, then off the heat add 2 tablespoons of butter cut into small pieces. Let it melt, whisking all the time, and when the emulsion begins, replace the saucepan over the heat and add the remaining 6 tablespoons of butter in bits, continuing to whisk. Never let the sauce come to a boil.

Finally, add 1 tablespoon cream at room temperature and about 4 tablespoons of the shrimp butter and beat until the velvety mixture is homogeneous.

To serve, unmold the custards onto hot plates. Reheat the shrimp in the sauce and put two on each plate, then spoon sauce over everything.

NOTE : This rather complicated recipe can be made easier if you prepare the shrimp cooking liquid and the shrimp butter the day before, then make the custard and finish the sauce on the day you are serving them. You can make the custard up to 3 hours ahead and keep it warm in the bain marie.

SALMIS DE GRIVE
Ragout of thrush

♫ ♫ ♫

Meat sauce

1 tablespoon butter
1 tablespoon olive oil
1 onion, minced
1 large clove garlic, minced
1 onion stuck with a clove
2 pounds chopped beef
1 small can (4 ounces) tomato
  sauce

1 cup dry white wine
1 bouquet garni (thyme, bay
  leaf, parsley, 2 stalks celery)
salt and pepper
5 juniper berries, roughly
  crushed

Melt the butter with the olive oil in a large saucepan and add the minced onions, the garlic, and the onion stuck with a clove. Cook until they begin to take on color, then add the chopped meat. Mix, then brown until the mass begins to stick, almost to caramelize. Your goal is to brown the meat without burning it and to develop the flavors. When it is ready, add the tomato sauce, mix, and stir in ½ cup of the white wine, the bouquet garni, and salt and pepper. Keep cooking, stirring constantly, until the meat almost caramelizes again.

Add the rest of the wine, and water to cover the meat, then add the juniper berries and cook over low heat for 3 hours.

Cooking the thrush
18 thrush
4 ounces (1 stick) butter

Leave the birds whole and uneviscerated with their heads and feet on, but plucked. Cook them in a frying pan with the butter, just to stiffen. When they begin to take on color, remove them.

Slit them along the length of their backs and take out their intestines. Discard the feet and the gizzard and set aside the liver, heart, lungs, and head and neck. Grind these in a mortar and pestle or food processor, then add to the meat sauce and cook for another 30 minutes.

Enrichment
3 tablespoons butter
⅓ cup flour
½ cup Madeira

Strain the sauce and press the residue in the strainer to get out all the juices. Pour a spoonful of boiling water through the residue into the sauce, then discard the solids. Taste the sauce and add 2 or 3 more crushed juniper berries if it needs them.

In another small saucepan, make a white roux with 3 tablespoons butter and the flour. Stir into the sauce with the Madeira and return it to a boil.

Arrange the re-formed thrushes in a saucepan so they don't overlap, cover them with sauce, and cook for 10 minutes. While they are cooking trim the crusts off 18 slices of white bread. Butter the bread and toast it in the oven.

Serve each thrush on a toast round on a hot serving platter with sauce spooned over it.

You can cook woodcock, hung at least 4 days, the same way.

N o t e s : Unless you are being really authentic you need not grind the heads of the thrush into the sauce—just discard them with the feet and gizzards.

This sauce is very good on squab, too. Cook them in butter in a frying pan until they are done but still rare, then continue with the recipe as is, cooking them for a final 20 minutes (because they are bigger) in the sauce.

QUASI DE VEAU AU LAIT
Roast veal in milk

𝒮𝒮𝒮

SERVES 6 TO 8

5-pound shoulder of veal,
  boned, rolled, and tied
4 cups scalded milk, cold
1 tablespoon olive oil

2 cloves garlic
salt and pepper
1 tablespoon good bourbon
½ cup Madeira

Mix together everything but the Madeira in a large, non-metal bowl, and let the veal marinate for a day or two in the refrigerator, turning it two or three times.

Put the veal and marinade in an ovenproof casserole and place in a cold oven, uncovered. Set the oven for 350°F. and cook for 2 hours. Watch closely so that the milk, at the beginning, doesn't boil over. After 2 hours lower the oven to 325°F. and cook, turning the meat from time to time, until the milk is almost evaporated but the residue has gilded the meat. Remove the meat and keep it warm while you remove the fat from the casserole. Then add the Madeira, stirring up the juices from the bottom of the pot. If you aren't going to serve immediately you can return the meat to the casserole and keep warm in a turned-off oven until you are ready.

Present the veal sliced, with the sauce spooned over it, accompanied with a purée of celeriac, p. 290.

PAQUETOUN DE BIOU
Stuffed scallops of beef

✿✿✿

SERVES 6

12 small beef scallops cut from
the point of the rump steak
10 ounces fresh ham (or any
fresh pork: chops, loin, etc.)
2 tablespoons chopped parsley
1 clove garlic
4½ ounces black olives
(preferably oil-cured)

1 tablespoon olive oil
3 tomatoes, peeled, seeded, and
chopped
18 small white onions, peeled
2 tablespoons Smyrna (golden)
raisins
1 pinch thyme
salt and pepper

Ask your butcher to cut very thin scallops about 3 by 6 inches
and to pound them flat. Trim them all to the same size and
save the trimmings. Grind the trimmings with the ham,
parsley, garlic, and olives. Spread some of this filling on
each beef scallop, roll the scallop around the filling, and tie
into a not too tight bundle.

Heat the olive oil in a cast-iron casserole large enough
to hold all the bundles in one layer. Brown over moderate
heat, then add the tomatoes, onions, raisins, and thyme. Salt
lightly and pepper. Bring to a boil.

Cover the casserole and cook over very low heat for
about 1½ hours. At the end of the cooking the rolls will be
swathed in a very thick sauce, a veritable fragrant, shimmer-
ing marmalade. If, while they are cooking, the beef seems
to be drying out too quickly, add a spoonful or so of hot
water.

Serve with fresh buttered noodles or gnocchi or French
spoonbread (see following recipe).

PURÉE DE MAÏS GRATINÉE
French spoonbread

𝒟 𝒟 𝒟

SERVES 6

4⅓ cups milk
1½ cups cornmeal
2 ounces (½ stick) butter
1¾ cups crème fraîche
salt and pepper

Preheat the oven to 425°F.

Lightly salt the milk and bring it to a boil. Sprinkle in all the cornmeal. Cook, stirring with a wire whisk, until the cornmeal has absorbed the milk and is the consistency of almost-dry mush.

Soften the mush by stirring in the butter, then the crème fraîche, adding it 1 tablespoon at a time until the mixture is the consistency of a thick paste but will still run when you tip the pot.

Taste and correct the seasoning and add a little pepper. Turn the mixture into a shallow, ovenproof 5-by-9-inch or 7-inch-square baking dish, and smooth the surface. Place in a hot (425°F.) oven for about 20 minutes or until the top is browned. Serve hot.

UNE DAUBE EN TROIS ÉPISODES
A three-episode beef casserole

🖉🖉🖉

SERVES 8

3½ pounds beef chuck, in
    stewing pieces
1¼ pounds beef round, in
    stewing pieces

Marinade

salt and pepper	1 bottle Gigondas or other
1 bay leaf	rough Rhône wine
2 cloves garlic	1 tablespoon olive oil
2 carrots, cut into large rounds	1 tablespoon dried orange peel
1 onion, minced	

Place all the meat pieces in a large nonmetal bowl. Mix together the ingredients for the marinade and pour over the meat. Let marinate for 48 hours, stirring two or three times.

Remove the meat from the marinade and dry it, then brown it in a little oil in a casserole over medium heat. Pour in all the marinade from the bowl, cover the casserole, and simmer for 3 hours.

The next day simmer for another 3 hours, adding a little water if the sauce seems too thick. But remember that thickness and velvetiness are what make a good daube—one that has cooked 4–5 hours.

Serve with the buttered noodles cooked *al dente*.

NOTE: This daube gets better with each reheating, but thin it with water as necessary.

PURÉE DE CÉLERIS RAVES
Purée of celeriac

♫ ♫ ♫

SERVES 6

3 large celeriacs	2 cups milk
juice of 2 lemons	salt and pepper
about 1 pound potatoes	nutmeg
2 tablespoons flour	4 ounces (1 stick) butter

Peel the celeriac and sprinkle it with lemon juice as you go along to keep it from turning brown. Slice it into thin circles. Weigh the celeriac and add one-quarter the weight in peeled potatoes (if the celeriac weighs 4 pounds add 1 pound of potatoes).

Dissolve the flour in a little water and lemon juice. In a large kettle bring 12 cups of salted water to a boil, then stir in the dissolved flour. Add the celeriac and potatoes and when the water returns to a boil cook at gentle boil for 30–40 minutes. Test; the celeriac should be easily crushed with the back of a fork.

Drain and purée. Stir in the milk, salt, pepper, nutmeg, and butter.

If the purée is too liquid, return it to a pot and cook, stirring constantly, over low heat until it dries out.

N O T E : This is also very good made with Jerusalem artichokes.

MOUSSE AU CHOCOLAT
DE TANTE YVONNE
Aunt Yvonne's chocolate mousse

SS SS SS

SERVES 6

2 oranges
10 ounces (2½ sticks) butter,
  softened
½ cup sugar
10 ounces bittersweet chocolate
6 eggs, separated

Grate the zest from the oranges into a bowl, add the butter and the sugar, then cream them all together.

Break or cut the chocolate into pieces and place in a heavy saucepan with the juice of the 2 oranges. Heat slowly, and when the chocolate has melted, stir to absorb all the juice, then let it bubble once or twice.

Off the heat add the egg yolks one at a time, beating each with a wire whisk to make sure it is absorbed before adding the next. When they have all been added, stir in the creamed butter.

Keep stirring until the mixture is almost cool, and then beat the egg whites until they form stiff peaks. Then fold them very carefully into the chocolate mixture. Lift the chocolate from the bottom and fold it over the whites, being careful not to beat.

Turn the mousse out into a serving bowl, cover with plastic wrap, and refrigerate (don't freeze) for at least 8 hours.

N o t e : This tastes like fruit-filled chocolates.

MADAME TRAMA

Tante Madée
Paris 6ᵉ

If Madame Trama, Tante Madée, practiced her art in China her Chinese hosts would think they were tasting French cooking. In Paris her creations are all a refinement of Chinese cooking—the real thing, the kind which very few gourmets know—but with local produce.

"My dishes are bouquets of flowers in season. The technique, that's the recipe."

Undisciplined, she is incapable, she says, of doing the same thing the same way twice. She never weighs anything, doesn't measure. Her eyes, her fingertips, don't miss. Nor does her taste.

When she sends forth from her kitchen her astonishing hot crabmeat mousse, its centerpiece of multiple greens baked into the mass and minced red cabbage pieces negligently—it seems—scattered around it, even a starving person wouldn't throw himself on it without admiring it first. She thinks of this arrangement of food as the Japanese do—as a symbol and a message.

Because this woman, working alone to order, perfects her work and presents it with art, you understand that the wait is necessarily long and you are patient. You will be rewarded.

She revolts against the ostracism which has kept women out of restaurant kitchens. Outspokenly she declares: "Women vote, they go to college, even to the polytechniques. But to learn cooking at a 'male' cooking school—no. The door is slammed in our faces.

"If really necessary, and if you already have a restaurant, you can spend several days with a *confrère* who will officiate before you. You will understand since you already speak his language. Experience—you have to get that on your own."

Calmed down, she went on to talk about herself and her vacation. Finally, reluctantly, she explained to me several of her recipes, underlining that she would be irritated at the least intrusion of my personality in their transcription. Here they are, faithfully reported, seductive Tante Madée.

FEUILLETÉS D'OURSINS AUX AVOCATS
Sea urchins in puff paste shells with avocado

ℐℐℐ

SERVES 4

12 large sea urchins, or 1 pound sea scallops
5 ounces pâte feuilletée, unsweetened
2 shallots, minced
2 sprigs tarragon
2 teaspoons white vermouth
1 cup champagne
1¼ cups heavy cream

4 ounces (1 stick) butter, cut into pieces
3 ripe avocados
1 pinch cayenne
chervil, chopped
juice of 1 lemon
2 teaspoons port, plus a little extra to marinate chives, minced

Carefully open the urchins. Set the coral aside in a small bowl on the stove to stay warm and put the urchins and their liquid in a small saucepan. If you use scallops put them in a saucepan with a little clam juice. Poach the seafood in their liquid for 2–3 minutes, just until done, then remove from heat but leave in the liquid to stay warm.

Preheat oven to 425°F.

Roll the pâte feuilletée into an 8-inch square, then cut into quarters. Bake in a hot oven until risen and golden (about 20–25 minutes), then remove from the oven and set aside to stay warm.

In a skillet heat the shallots, tarragon, vermouth, champagne, and 1½ tablespoons of the seafood poaching liquid. Reduce over moderate heat until it is syrupy, then add half the cream (½ cup plus 2 tablespoons) and reduce some more, to half. Strain, then off the heat stir in the butter a piece at a time. Return to heat and keep the sauce warm, but don't let it boil again.

Purée two of the avocados—the purée should be very smooth. Reserve the third. Add a pinch of cayenne and the chopped chervil to the purée. Heat with a tablespoon of cream, several squirts of lemon juice, and 2 teaspoons port. Add more cream if the mixture is too thick. Stir to make it very smooth. Add this purée to the sauce.

Using a melon baller, make small balls out of the flesh of the remaining avocado and let them heat in a little port, while you finish the recipe.

Open the pastry puffs as you would a biscuit, around the equator. Sprinkle the coral on the bottoms and spoon the sauce evenly over them. Put in the urchins or scallops and top with the pastry covers. Arrange on a plate, surround with the avocado balls, and sprinkle with the minced chives.

CANARD AUX FIGUES ET AUX FRAMBOISES
Duck with figs and raspberries

SERVES 4

16 fresh black figs

3⅛ cups Bordeaux

salt

cinnamon

1 sprig lemon verbena flower

juice of 1 orange

pepper

8 ounces raspberries (½-pint box)

2 ducklings, 3–3½ pounds each

3 tablespoons brandy

1 tablespoon sugar

juice of 1 lemon

2 tablespoons wine vinegar

2 ounces (½ stick) butter, cut into pieces

Prick the figs lightly with a skewer or fork and marinate for 3 hours in the wine, with a pinch of salt and cinnamon, the verbena, 1 tablespoon of the orange juice, and 2 grinds of pepper.

Crush the raspberries into a purée and set aside at room temperature.

Roast the ducks in a 400°F. oven, turning them frequently, for 1 hour. Remove them from the oven and cut them into serving pieces, detaching the fillets with the legs and wings. Catch any juices or blood rendered during the carving and reserve it along with the carcasses. Pour a little juice over the ducks and set aside to keep warm.

Slice the figs and arrange them on an ovenproof dish. Save the marinade. Cover the figs with buttered waxed paper or foil and heat in a very slow oven (the one you are keeping the ducks hot in is fine). It is important that they be hot while keeping their natural color. You should also be heating the raspberry purée, either in the same oven or in a pot on the stove.

Chop up the duck carcasses and return them to the roasting pan. Heat the brandy, then pour it over the carcasses in the roasting pan and flame. Sprinkle with the sugar. Mix in the rest of the orange juice, the lemon juice, and the vinegar. Stirring, reduce until the liquid caramelizes, and then add 2½ cups of the fig-marinade wine. Bring to a boil and let the sauce simmer and clarify itself. If it doesn't, skim off any impurities that rise to the top. Strain through a fine sieve.

Return to the heat and add the reserved duck juices. Just before the sauce reaches a boil add, bit by bit, the butter pieces. Keep beating as you add the butter to bind the sauce, and don't let it boil.

On a large, hot platter arrange the duck legs, the wings, and the fillets, sliced into strips. (Each person should be served half a duck.) Spoon the sauce over the duck, then surround it with a ring of overlapping slices of hot figs. Pour the raspberry purée around the outside edge of the ring of figs.

LES PETITS LÉGUMES DE TANTE MADÉE
Aunt Madée's tiny vegetables

𝒮𝒮𝒮

SERVES 6

12 little new carrots
12 little new turnips
1 cup fresh green beans, the
  younger the better
1 cup fresh peas
1 pound fresh wild mushrooms,
  or domestic mushrooms, the
  smaller the better
2 tablespoons flour
juice of 1 lemon
4–6 artichoke bottoms
  (depending on their size)

1 cucumber
6 tablespoons (¾ stick) butter
1 sprig thyme, or ½ teaspoon
  powdered
1 bay leaf
salt and pepper
fresh herbs of the season or
  fresh mint
2 tablespoons heavy cream

Peel the carrots and the turnips and slice into rounds about
1 inch thick for the carrots, ¾ inch thick for the turnips.
Toss into a lot of boiling salted water. Add the beans if they
are large and mature, but leave them raw if they are young
beans. The same with the peas. Or, if they are medium-size,
add partway through the cooking; use your own judgment.
When the water returns to the boil, adjust the heat so it is
simmering. Remove the vegetables from the water after 10
minutes.

If the mushrooms are large, cut them into two or three
pieces.

This may seem fussy but all these precautions are
necessary to the charm of this dish.

Add the flour and lemon juice to the pot of boiling salted water and poach the artichoke bottoms. Remove them when they are still somewhat crunchy. Slice the artichokes and cucumber, but slice the artichokes a bit thicker.

Melt the butter in a large skillet with high sides, a *sautoir* if you have one, and put in all the vegetables along with the thyme and bay leaf. Over low heat let the vegetables exchange aromas more than really cook, and evaporate any liquid they might exude. Salt and pepper moderately.

When the mixture seems coated in glistening juices, add the herbs or mint and the cream. Be judicious in your use of herbs. Let the cream reduce over moderate heat.

All the vegetables should be crunchy and combine to make a mixture without sauce but sparkling in their own juices.

Serve with anything—roasts, sweetbreads, or broiled meats—in little side dishes.

MARINETTE VACHERON

Le Râtelier
Lyon 1er

Marinette Vacheron's place is not where to go for a Big Feed—it's a restaurant.

It's a prewar setting. Packed-together tables separated by tastefully arranged bouquets. Thirty places at most, a well-polished counter, a collection of oil lamps and copper candlesticks on étagères. It's hot, bright, welcoming.

"At my place everything is simple—no potatoes cut and colored like roses, no napkins twisted up into the shape of gondolas," said she, laughing.

"My husband and I have worked in famous places and it's an enriching sort of school. My menu is small, seasonal, and according to what's in the markets."

Classical lyonnaise cuisine with a contemporary touch: porgies cooked to perfection with fresh noodles made by Marinette and served *al dente, osso bucco* with wild mushrooms, all local fish.

In game season she ventures forth with hare à la royale, with salmis of wild birds. A flight over her repertoire would be incomplete without vegetables. Her tomatoes can't really be called "provençale"—they are baked in her oven. Her zucchini, green beans, artichoke bottoms, and asparagus, that vegetable so often neglected even in the best places, are savory, unadorned, cooked just to crunchy tenderness and far from the often-served limp stalks.

Barely seated, you can judge her refinements with her hors d'oeuvres. A big platter adorned with leaves of red lettuce, grated carrots, little green beans, hard-boiled eggs, red beets, celery rémoulade, olives, and I forget what else, except four white, parsley-sprinkled milestones. They are boiled potatoes, served still hot to help you appreciate the marinated herring fillets and the anchovy fillets in oil served generously in their terrine. I had no room for the charcuterie.

One of Marinette's revelations: "pigeons ficelés." Packets of bacon rind, entirely degreased and rolled to make a *boudin*, then introduced into simmered dishes as a way to thicken the sauce and give it a velvety texture without a liaison or to assure a natural jellying for braised meats to be served cold.

MES DAURADES AUX NOUILLES
Porgies with noodles

✧✧✧

SERVES 6

3 porgies, about 1½–2 pounds each
salt and pepper
1 cup dry white vermouth
1¼ cups heavy cream
7 ounces fresh sorrel, cut with
    scissors into very fine strips

Ask your fish store to remove the fillets from both sides of the fish, leave them in one piece, and skin them.

Preheat oven to 400°F.

Arrange the unadorned pieces of fish on an ovenproof dish so that they don't overlap and place in the oven for 8–10 minutes.

Keep them warm without cooking any longer. Salt and pepper lightly.

While the fish is cooking, reduce the cup of vermouth to a syrup over medium heat, then add the cream. Reduce some more until the sauce coats a wooden spoon. Add pepper, then begin adding the sorrel, little by little, so you can judge (by your taste) when you have added enough. Bring to a boil, salt if necessary, then remove from the heat.

Arrange the fish fillets on a heated serving platter, spoon the sauce over them, and serve.

Homemade noodles, cooked *al dente* and served buttered, make a very nice accompaniment.

NOTE: If you can't find porgies, you can substitute sea bream.

Paquetoun de biou
(Escalopes de bœuf farcies)

12 escalopes

Farce

persil

huile   ail   jambon cru   olives noires
d'olive

Cuisson

oignons   cocotte   raisins secs

tomates

Canard aux figues et aux framboises

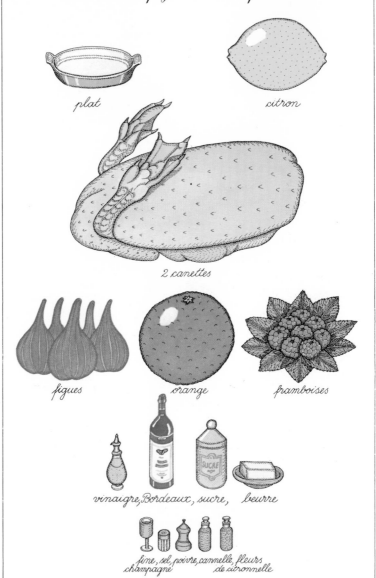

plat

citron

2 canettes

figues

orange

framboises

vinaigre, Bordeaux, sucre, beurre

fine, sel, poivre, cannelle, fleurs
champagne   de citronnelle

LOTTE AU COULIS D'ÉTRILLES
Bellyfish in crab sauce

✍ ✍ ✍

SERVES 6

3½ pounds live crabs
½ cup cognac, warmed
4 ounces (1 stick) butter
2 tablespoons chopped shallots
1 bouquet garni (thyme,
    parsley, bay leaf)

1 bottle white Mâconnais wine
½ cup heavy cream
salt and pepper
paprika or cayenne
2½ pounds bellyfish

Begin with the sauce. Wash the crabs well, drain them, and drop them into a kettle. Sprinkle with the warmed cognac and flame them to kill them. Cut them in half, and crack their claws.

Melt half the butter in a large, heavy-bottomed saucepan, and cook the shallots until they are soft, but not brown. Add the crabs, the bouquet garni, and the wine, which should come level with the top of the contents of the saucepan. Cook at a low boil for 25–30 minutes.

Strain, but reserve and set aside the liquid. Crush the crabs in a mortar and pestle, then put through the coarse blade of a food mill. Put through again at the medium blade, then push through a sieve, moistening with the set-aside liquid as you push it through. This will gather up all the cooking juices. Or purée in a food processor and then put through a sieve with the juices.

Over moderate heat reduce to 1 cup, then add the cream and reduce some more until it is the consistency of melted ice cream. Add salt and pepper and a little pinch of strong paprika or cayenne and the rest of the butter, beating constantly as you add it. Do not let the sauce boil again, but keep it warm while you cook the fish.

Slice the bellyfish into serving pieces and toss into a kettle of salted boiling water. Lower the heat and let the fish poach, without boiling, until it can be pierced easily with a fork, but isn't soft. Drain.

Serve with the sauce spooned over it.

N o t e : A good fish man can order bellyfish for you, but you can also substitute any firm-fleshed fish such as halibut, whiting, or cod.

JARRET DE VEAU AUX MOUSSERONS
Veal shanks with mushrooms

✐ ✐ ✐

SERVES 4

4 ounces (1 stick) butter
4 veal shanks
1 small piece lean bacon rind
salt and pepper
1 pound wild mushrooms,
   washed and dried

Melt the butter in a casserole large enough so that all the shanks can lie in one layer. Then, over moderate heat, brown the shanks with the bacon rind. Add salt and pepper. Cover and let simmer for 20–25 minutes, then turn the meat over and top with the mushrooms.

Cover the pot again and let cook until the meat is falling off the bones, about 1½ hours. Remove the rind and serve with Baker's Wife potatoes (following recipe).

NOTES: The veal shanks may be left in one big piece, but they will be easier to handle if you ask your butcher to saw them into rounds about 2 inches long. Ask him to cut them as he would for *osso bucco*.

Although wild mushrooms are delicious in this dish, you can perfectly well substitute commercial domestic ones, which will be almost as good. If you use dried wild mushrooms, soak them before adding them to the pot.

POMMES BOULANGÈRE
Baker's Wife potatoes

𝒟 𝒟 𝒟

2¼ pounds (about 5 medium)
  potatoes
1 onion, minced
salt and pepper
4 ounces (1 stick) butter

Preheat oven to 400°F.

Peel the potatoes, then slice them into very thin rounds as for potato chips. Dry them well, mix them with the minced onion, and add salt and pepper.

Arrange in layers in a well-buttered gratin dish (use about a quarter of the butter for this), then pour in water just to cover the potatoes. Dot the top with the rest of the butter.

Bake until most of the water has evaporated and only the butter is left—about 45 minutes. Then lower the heat and let the top of the potatoes brown. If you think they are browning too fast, cover the top with a piece of waxed paper.

The whole process will take more than an hour of cooking.

N O T E : Don't peel and slice the potatoes until just before you are ready to cook them or they will turn a nasty brown. And even though they will brown in the oven, the dish will look unappetizing.

CIVET DE BOEUF
Beef stew

✑ ✑ ✑

SERVES 6

3½ pounds boned short ribs
10 ounces pork fatback
4 ounces lean bacon rind, rolled
   and tied
3 medium onions, halved
2 shallots
1 clove garlic

1 bouquet garni (parsley,
   thyme, bay leaf)
pepper
white of 1 large leek
1 bottle Beaujolais Villages
1 tablespoon olive oil
½ cup pork blood (see note)

Cut the boned ribs into small pieces, about 1-inch cubes, and the fatback into a matchstick julienne. Place them in a bowl with the rolled bacon rind. Add the onions, shallots, and garlic, peeled but whole, the bouquet garni, 6 grinds of pepper, and the white of the leek cut in half the long way. Pour in the wine and olive oil and mix well.

Let marinate in the refrigerator for 8 hours.

Strain, reserving the marinade. Pick out the pieces of fatback and render them slowly in a large iron casserole. When they have given off their fat and are little crisps, discard the fat and put everything else into the casserole, including the strained wine. Bring to a boil, cover, and let simmer for 2½ hours over very low heat. Check on how the meat is cooking; it should be very tender and the sauce relatively scant.

Meanwhile prepare the polenta (see below), which can

be made well ahead of time and left in the refrigerator until the final heating.

Just before you are going to serve the stew, scoop out half a cup of the sauce and heat it with the blood in a small pot. Bring it to a boil, then immediately take it off the heat. Add to the stew, bring just to the verge of a boil, then remove instantly lest the blood congeal. Remove the bouquet garni and the rind and serve with the polenta.

Polenta gratinée

1⅔ cups yellow cornmeal
4 ounces (1 stick) butter
¼ cup grated Parmesan cheese
nutmeg (optional, but good)
3 tablespoons grated Gruyère or
    Swiss cheese

In a large pot bring 8 cups lightly salted water to a rolling boil. Sprinkle in the cornmeal all at once, stirring with a whisk to break up any lumps. Let thicken over low heat, stirring constantly with a whisk or wooden spoon. Cook for 30 minutes. All cornmeal doesn't absorb the same way, so have some boiling water ready, which you can add if the cornmeal mush seems to be getting too thick. It should be the consistency of good porridge.

After it has cooked for 30 minutes stir in the butter, Parmesan cheese, and a pinch of nutmeg, if you like it.

Pour out into a large, flat, ovenproof dish such as a 15-by-10-inch rectangular cake pan.

Sprinkle the grated cheese over the top and dot with butter.

It is at this stage that you can set the polenta aside,

covered with a piece of waxed paper, until 30 minutes before you are ready to serve. Then it should be placed in a pre-heated 400°F. oven for 30 minutes or until the top is lightly browned.

Note: The blood is to thicken the stew. If you can't get it, or would rather not use it, you can obtain the same effect by blending together ½ stick butter with ¼ cup flour, then stirring this beurre manie into the almost boiling stew just before you serve.

RIZ PAIMPOLAISE
Rice with vegetables

ℐℐℐ

SERVES 6

This rice is an excellent accompaniment for fish, meats with sauces, roasts, etc.

3 fresh medium artichokes
1 tablespoon flour
4 ounces (1 stick) butter,
   melted
2 cups long-grain rice

1 cup fresh peas
1 cup very tiny green beans
   cut into ½-inch pieces
salt and pepper

To prepare the artichokes, first pull off the tough leaves around the stem until you have a cone with a "waist." This will be just above the bulge before the inner leaves rise to a point. Cut through the "waist" with a sharp knife. At this stage leave the choke and the stem and leaf ends, which can be removed more easily after the artichoke is cooked.

Stir the flour into 2 quarts of salted cold water and bring to a boil. Add the trimmed artichokes and cook until they are tender but still crunchy. They shouldn't be allowed to get mushy. This should take 10–15 minutes, depending on size.

Remove the artichokes from the water and with a sharp knife scrape out the bristly chokes, then cut off the stems and trim off all the rough parts left on the bottoms. Cut each into eight pieces and set aside in the melted butter.

Bring 5 cups of salted water to a boil and add the rice.

Let boil, uncovered, for 5 minutes, then add the peas and the beans and continue to cook, still uncovered. When the water is almost evaporated add the artichoke bottoms and the butter, and salt and pepper. When the rice is cooked *al dente*, there shouldn't be any water left in the pot. If there is, dry it out in the oven or over very low heat after having added the artichokes and butter.

For this dish the rice should be chewy and the vegetables still firm.

NOTE : This dish can also be made with frozen vegetables. Frozen artichoke bottoms (not hearts) are an especially satisfactory substitute for fresh. Don't use canned or bottled unless you are sure they haven't been preserved in oil. Add the peas and beans frozen, and cook according to the recipe, but thaw the artichoke bottoms before adding with the butter.

JANINE VOIZENET

La Vieille Auberge
Saint-Agnan (Nièvre)

The old inn came out of its cosmetic operation without ill effects. On the contrary it is now young, spruce, flourishing.

Janine Voizenet has also renovated the interior. Her dining room deserves the same complimentary adjectives as the façade. The napkins, yellow and mauve bouquets in the glasses, are evidence of a touching desire to please.

Finally, Janine appears: mature, smiling, engaging, exuding the good smells of her kitchen. This is an all-new, vast, functional, commodious kitchen. A large window is open above the vault of a baking oven which looks like a stage set: rabbit rillettes in an enormous cauldron giving up a belch now and then, testimony to their slow cooking.

Here there is no prettification. The huge table is loaded with leeks, carrots, all the vegetables that are going into a stew with a piece of pork and various charcuteries especially prepared by the neighborhood charcutier. It will be a stew with three pigs' feet, which will give it the "morvandiot" flavor, says Janine, with that trace of an accent which sings of the Morvan country.

The handsome perch at the end of the table flaps its tail in protest. They are looking for a dish big enough to put it into the oven swimming in cream. They are worried because the butcher hasn't delivered the fillet of Charolais beef yet. Then Janine takes from the refrigerator her ball of puff paste to give it its last turn. The fillet will be *en croûte*. It's an order. "They want my flan, too." Another Morvan specialty.

Janine has created her personal ones. Such as packets of rabbit meat en gelée, her sumptuous rillettes, always on hand to help guests wait, and her famous ham tart—beautiful golden crust that looks like a dessert but is really a soothing hot first course.

The recipe: "I don't weigh anything—how do you want me to explain to you? You have to play with cups and spoons to guess the proportions."

RILLETTES DE LAPIN
Rabbit pâté

SST ST ST

Janine Voizenet makes her rillettes from the forequarters of rabbits and serves them with the saddles, roasted.

2¼ pounds rabbit forequarters
2¼ pounds unsmoked, fatty
   bacon, in 1-inch cubes
1 bouquet garni (parsley,
   thyme, bay leaf)
2 cloves garlic

2 carrots, sliced the long way
salt and pepper
1 clove
1 bottle dry white wine, such as
   Aligoté

In a heavy kettle combine the rabbit forequarters, including the heads, with the cubed bacon, the bouquet garni, the garlic, carrots, salt and pepper, and clove. Make a mixture of two-thirds wine to one-third cold water and add it to the kettle to cover the meat and come about ¼ inch above it.

Bring to a boil, cover, and simmer over very low heat for 7–8 hours.

Let cool. Strain the cooking liquid. Carefully, using your hands rather than a knife, take all the bones out of the rabbit. Discard the rabbit heads. Put the bacon pieces through the medium blade of a food mill or a food processor. Cut the rabbit meat into a small dice. Combine the meats and the strained juices in a large glass bowl, and correct the seasoning—make it quite strong. The taste of the rillettes depends on this, and it will become blander when it is chilled.

Set aside for 4–5 hours in a cool place. It will congeal.

Stir often to reincorporate the fat, which will rise to the top. When your pâté has a good consistency, put a piece of aluminum foil over the bowl and place in the refrigerator.

Remove from the refrigerator 1 or 2 hours before serving, depending on the temperature of the house. Serve with toast.

GARENNES EN GELÉE
Wild rabbits in aspic

ℐℐℐ

3 boned wild rabbits

Marinade

3 carrots
10 peppercorns
salt
1 bouquet garni (parsley,
    thyme, bay leaf)
1 bottle dry white wine, such as
    Aligoté, Chablis, etc.

Gelée

heads and all the bones of the
    rabbits
2 carrots
2 onions
1 clove garlic

1 bouquet garni (parsley,
    thyme, bay leaf)
salt and pepper
dried truffles

Cut the rabbits apart into pieces.

Bone the pieces without tearing the flesh. Set aside the bones and heads. Wrap the flesh into bundles about the size of tangerines and tie them up.

Arrange the bundles in a large bowl with all the marinade ingredients, then set aside in a cool place for a maximum of 24 hours. Turn the bundles two or three times, being careful they don't come apart.

Place in a heavy casserole large enough so the bundles don't touch each other and cover with the marinade. Add more wine if necessary. Cook, covered, at a low simmer for 5–6 hours, then let cool to cold.

While the rabbit is cooking, combine the rabbit heads and bones with the carrots, onions, garlic, bouquet garni, salt, and pepper, and cook in about 8 cups of water to make a gelatin.

Cut the strings off the bundles of rabbit meat and arrange the meat in a serving bowl. Degrease the cooking juices and strain it, then strain the gelée and combine the two.

Pour over the meat. Sprinkle with a few pinches of dried truffles for flavoring. Refrigerate for 8–10 hours and serve when the gelatin is set.

NOTE: If you are using a prepackaged or frozen rabbit and don't have the head, or are squeamish, you can make the gelée with unflavored gelatin. Follow directions with the bones you have and cook them with the seasonings to get a well-flavored base, then after the gelée and the cooking liquid have been strained, but before they have been combined, add 1 envelope of gelatin (¼ ounce) for every 2 cups of liquid. Chill according to directions.

CAKE AU JAMBON
Ham cake

SSS

FOR A 9-BY-6-INCH CAKE PAN

7 tablespoons flour, measured
  then sifted

3 eggs

⅓ cup cold milk

¼ cup oil

9 ounces cooked ham, diced

⅓ cup grated Gruyère or Swiss
  cheese

1 tablespoon baking powder

1 tablespoon butter

In a bowl, work the sifted flour into the eggs until the mixture bubbles. Add the milk, mixing as you go, then the oil, adding the same way. Finally mix together the diced ham, the grated cheese, and the baking powder and stir them in, too.

Stir and knead the dough to aerate it and to complete the incorporation of the various elements.

Butter a pan, using the tablespoon of butter, then sprinkle with flour and tap to get rid of the excess. Turn the dough into the pan. It should fill it three-quarters full. Let rest in a warm place for 15 minutes.

While it is resting preheat the oven to 400°F.

Put the cake into the oven, and then don't open the oven door for 20 minutes. After that time check the color and if it is browning too quickly cover with waxed paper.

The cooking should take 35–40 minutes altogether. Test to see if the cake is done by sticking the point of a knife into it. The point should come out clean. Don't snatch the cake out of the oven immediately. Leave it there for several minutes with the heat off and the door open so the sudden cold air won't make it crack or fall.

Unmold on a rack and serve warm.

If you have leftover cake you can slice it and brown the slices in butter in a frying pan over moderate heat. Served with a seasonal salad, this makes a very agreeable last-minute dinner.

Index

ANGLETERRE

LA MANCHE

Marthe Fau
Auberge Saint Quent
Livry-Gar

Exmes
Simone Lemaire
"Le Tourne-Bride"

M. De Bernard
"Château de Teildras"
Cheffes-Sur-Sarthe

Ch
Gi
La

Saint
Janine
La Vieille

- Colette Maudonnet - "Aux Naulets D'Anjou" Gennes

- Marie-Jo Ferrand - Challans
"Le Gîte-Du-Tourne-Pierre"

Les Sables D'Olonne
Antoinette Léger. "Au Capitaine"

M. de Trama
"Tante Madée"

Fernande Allard
"Allard"

M. Cartet
"Restaurant Cartet"

Soubise
Liliane Benoît
"Le Soubise"

PARIS

Fernande Turet
"Le Pistou"

Georgette Descat
"Lous Landès"

Gastes

Paulette Arbulo
"L'Estanquet"

Dominique Nahmias
"Olympe"

Eauze
Huguette Meliet
"Moulin de Pouy"

Christiane Massia
"L'Aquitaine"

ESPAGNE